Revelations Revealed

The Church, The Conflict, The Conqueror

By

Harold Bryant

authorHOUSE

1663 LIBERTY DRIVE, SUITE 200
BLOOMINGTON, INDIANA 47403
(800) 839-8640
www.authorhouse.com

First published by AuthorHouse 07/22/04

ISBN: 1-4184-0057-2 (e-book)
ISBN: 1-4184-0058-0 (Paperback)

Library of Congress Control Number: 2003099370

This book is printed on acid free paper.

Printed in the United States of America
Bloomington, IN

CONTENTS:

INTRODUCTION

This book is written to try to simplify and to clarify the Book of Revelation. Scriptures from the whole Bible have been used to verify what has been written. Many people have written books on Revelation and many of them make the book seem like a mystery. The Book of Revelation is simple if you take it at face value. John's revelation on the Isle of Patmos was a divine encounter with God, foretelling the events leading up to the great and glorious day of the return of Christ our Lord and Savior for those redeemed by the blood of the Lamb.

This Book will make an excellent study guide. All scriptures are taken from the King James Version.

My prayer is that it will bless you through your walk with Christ.

CHAPTER 1

The Revelation of Jesus Christ, which God gave unto him, to shew unto his servants things which must shortly come to pass; and he sent and signified *it* by his angel unto his servant John:

2   Who bare record of the word of God, and of the testimony of Jesus Christ, and of all things that he saw.

3   Blessed *is* he that readeth, and they that hear the words of this prophecy, and keep those things which are written therein: for the time is at hand.

4   JOHN to the seven churches which are in Asia: Grace *be* unto you, and peace, from him which is, and which was, and which is to come; and from the seven Spirits which are before his throne;

5   And from Jesus Christ, who *is* the faithful witness, and the first begotten of the dead, and the prince of the Kings of the earth. Unto him that loved us, and washed us from our sins in his own blood,

6   And hath made us kings and priests unto God and his Father; to him *be* glory and domination for ever and ever. Amen.

7   Behold, he cometh with clouds; and every eye shall see him, and they *also* which pierced him: and all kindreds of the earth shall wail because of him. Even so, Amen.

8   I am Alpha and Omega, the beginning and the ending, saith the Lord, which is, and which was, and which is to come, the Almighty.

9   I John, who also am your brother, and companion in tribulation, and in the kingdom and patience of Jesus Christ, was in the isle that is called Patmos, for the word of God, and for the testimony of Jesus Christ.

10   I was in the Spirit on the Lord's day, and heard behind me a great voice, as of a trumpet,

11   Saying, I am Alpha and Omega, the first and the last: and, What thou seest, write in a book, and send *it* unto the seven churches which are in Asia; unto Eph'e-sus, and unto Smyrna, and unto Per'ga-mos, and unto Thy-a-ti'ra, and unto Sardis, and unto Philadelphia, and unto La-od-i-ce'a.

12   And I turned to see the voice that spake with me. And being turned, I saw seven golden candlesticks;

13   And in the midst of the seven candlesticks *one* like unto the Son of man, clothed with a garment down to the foot, and girt about the paps with a golden girdle.

14 His head and *his* hairs were white like wool, as white as snow; and his eyes *were* as a flame of fire;

15 And his feet like unto fine brass, as if they burned in a furnace; and his voice as the sound of many waters.

16 And he had in his right hand seven stars: and out of his mouth went a sharp twoedged sword: and his countenance *was* as the sun shineth in his strength.

17 And when I saw him, I fell at his feet as dead. And he laid his right hand upon me, saying unto me, Fear not; I am the first and the last:

18 I *am* he that liveth, and was dead; and, behold, I am alive for evermore, Amen; and have the keys of hell and of death.

19 Write the things which thou hast seen, and the things which are, and the things which shall be hereafter;

20 The mystery of the seven stars which thou sawest in my right hand, and the seven golden candlesticks. The seven stars are the angels of the seven churches: and the seven candlesticks which thou sawest are the seven churches.

Chapter 1

Introduction of Christ and his church

This Book is a Revelation of Jesus Christ. It is His story. He is the main character of this book. Not the devil or beast or false prophet. Jesus Christ the Lamb of God slain for the sins of the world now will take center stage in this book. He will be the one to open every seal, set the bounds for every judgment, give power to all the characters or take it away. He is on every page fulfilling every word of prophecy. I believe He said it very well in verses 17, 18. Fear Not I am the first and the last and was dead and behold; I am alive forevermore, amen: and have the keys of hell and death.

There is a blessing to read or hear the words of this Book. But the real blessing is to keep the words that you do hear. Now is the time to do it. When these words were written it was AD 96. Now it is 2003. The time is at hand, the day is far spent, and the night is upon us. We are entering the darkest time in our history, but there is a light at the end of the tunnel. Jesus will be there.

Jesus is the faithful witness, the only faithful witness. He has never failed. He loved us so much He washed our sins away in His own blood; making us Kings and Priests unto God.

What great heights His love has elevated us to.

Again He is telling us how He will come for us on a cloud with every eye looking at Him. This is what Matthew 24:27 tells us, for as the lightening cometh out of the east, and shineth even unto the west; so shall also the coming of the Son of Man be. Before Jesus left earth He told us something of great importance to assure His church that it could accomplish His task in this world and also how to look for Him. Acts 1:8-11; but ye shall receive power, after that the Holy Ghost has come upon you: and ye shall be witnesses unto me both in Jerusalem, and in all Judea, and in Samaria, and unto the uttermost part of the earth. And when he had spoken these things, while they beheld, he was taken up; and a cloud received him out of their sight. And while they looked steadfastly toward Heaven as He went up, behold, two men stood by them in white apparel; which also said, ye men of Galilee, why stand ye here gazing into Heaven? This same Jesus, who is taken up from you into Heaven, shall so come in like manner as ye have seen Him go into Heaven. The only place in this book that identified with these verses is found in Revelation 14:14-15. Notice the angel said the harvest of the earth is ripe. You save the harvest and burn the weeds. John was already beginning to experience what this book is about. He was being persecuted for his testimony. This is the last stand between good and evil and John was sharing in it. When John received this prophecy it was Sunday. After the resurrection, Sunday was always called the Lords day. He said I was in the Spirit, meaning his mind was on the things of God or he was praying in the Spirit. If you want to receive anything from God we have to be in the Spirit. This world cannot reveal anything to us. John hears a voice like a trumpet saying I am Alpha and Omega, the first and the last. What you are about to see write in a book and send it to the seven churches which are in Asia. Just about all these churches are located in Turkey around the Mediterranean Sea. These churches were picked because these seven contain every situation in all churches of all times. What went on in these churches is going to be common to all.

The Bible says that all temptations are common to all people. How we deal with them makes the difference. John said "I turned to see the voice that spoke with me, and being turned I saw seven golden candlesticks." Exodus 25:31 gives the directions for making the candlesticks. It was to be of pure gold, a large shaft in the middle with three smaller ones on each side of one single piece of gold. This lamp stand was to be placed in the Tabernacle. This was the only light in it. Also it was never to go out. Jesus was in the midst of them clothed with a garment down to his feet with a golden girdle about His chest. His hair was white as snow. His eyes were as a flame of fire: His feet like fine polished brass. His voice was like a great waterfall. We have never seen the Lord like this. No wonder John fell at His feet as dead. In His right hand were seven stars and from His mouth a sharp two edged sword. And over all He was shining like the sun in full strength. He laid His right hand upon John saying, "Fear not, I am the first and last. I was alive and was dead but behold I am alive forevermore. I also have the keys or the authority over hell and death." A command is given to write the things which he had saw and the things which are and also the things which shall be hereafter. Most people take the hereafter to mean after the church is gone. But I believe it means just what it says. The things that are going to happen after what you write about the seven churches.

Notice what Jesus said about the mystery of the seven stars and the seven golden candlesticks. The stars are the overseers and the candlesticks represent the seven churches. What was the mystery of the church that Jesus is talking about? This term is used again in Revelation 10:7. The mystery in Revelation 1:20 is the beginning of the church and in Revelation 10:7 it represents the end of the church. Ephesians 3:1-10 For this cause I Paul, the prisoner of Jesus Christ for you Gentiles, If ye have heard of the dispensation of the grace of God which is given me to you-ward: How that by revelation he made known unto me the mystery; (as I wrote afore in few words, Whereby, when ye read, ye may understand my knowledge in the mystery of Christ) Which in other ages was not made known unto the sons of men, as it is now revealed unto his holy apostles and prophets by the Spirit; That the gentiles should be fellow-heirs, and of the same body, and partakers of His promise in Christ by the gospel: Whereof I was made a minister, according to the gift of the grace of God given unto me by the effectual working of His power. Unto me, who am less than the least of all saints, is this grace given, that I should preach among the Gentiles the un-searchable riches of Christ; And to make all men see what is the fellowship of the mystery, which from the beginning of the world hath been hid in God, who created all things by Jesus Christ: To the intent that now unto the principalities and powers in heavenly places might be known by the church the manifold wisdom of God. This is more fully explained in Chapter 10 and verse 7.

CHAPTER 2

UNTO the angel of the church of Eph'e-sus write; These things saith he that holdeth the seven stars in his right hand, who walketh in the midst of the seven golden candlesticks;

2   I know thy works, and thy labour, and thy patience, and how thou canst not bear them which are evil: and thou hast tried them which say they are apostles, and are not, and hast found them liars:

3   And hast borne, and hast patience, and for my name's sake hast laboured, and hast not fainted.

4   Nevertheless I have *somewhat* against thee, because thou hast left thy first love.

5   Remember therefore from whence thou art fallen, and repent, and do the first works; or else I will come unto thee quickly, and will remove thy candlestick out of his place, except thou repent.

6   But this thou hast, that thou hatest the deeds of the Nic-o-la'i-tanes, which I also hate.

7   He that hath an ear, let him hear what the Spirit saith unto the churches; To him that overcometh will I give to eat of the tree of life, which is in the midst of the paradise of God.

8   And unto the angel of the church in Smyrna write; These things saith the first and the last, which was dead, and is alive;

9   I know thy works, and tribulation, and poverty, (but thou art rich) and I *know* the blasphemy of them which say they are Jews, and are not, but are the synagogue of Satan.

10   Fear none of those things which thou shalt suffer: behold, the devil shall cast *some* of you into prison, that ye may be tried; and ye shall have tribulation ten days: be thou faithful unto death, and I will give thee a crown of life.

11   He that hath an ear, let him hear what the Spirit saith unto the churches; He that overcometh shall not be hurt of the second death.

12   And to the angel of the church in Per'ga-mos write; These things saith he which hath the sharp sword with two edges;

13   I know thy works, and where thou dwellest, *even* where Satan's seat *is*: and thou holdest fast my name, and hast not denied my faith, even in those days wherein An'ti-pas *was* my faithful martyr, who was slain among you, where Satan dwelleth.

14   But I have a few things against thee, because thou hast there them that hold the doctrine of Ba'laam, who taught Balac to cast a

stumblingblock before the children of Israel, to eat things sacrificed unto idols, and to commit fornication.

15   So hast thou also them that hold the doctrine of the Nic-o-la'i-tanes, which thing I hate.

16   Repent; or else I will come unto thee quickly, and will fight against them with the sword of my mouth.

17   He that hath an ear, let him hear what the Spirit saith unto the churches; To him that overcometh will I give to eat of the hidden manna, and will give him a white stone, and in the stone a new name written, which no man knoweth saving he that receiveth *it*.

18   And unto the angel of the church in Thy-a-ti'ra write; These things saith the Son of God, who hath his eyes like unto a flame of fire, and his feet *are* like fine brass;

19   I know thy works, and charity, and service, and faith, and thy patience, and thy works; and the last to *be* more than the first.

20   Notwithstanding I have a few things against thee, because thou sufferest that woman Jez'e-bel, which calleth herself a prophetess, to teach and to seduce my servants to commit fornication, and to eat things sacrificed unto idols.

21   And I gave her space to repent of her fornication; and she repented not.

22   Behold, I will cast her into a bed, and them that commit adultery with her into great tribulation, except they repent of their deeds.

23   And I will kill her children with death; and all the churches shall know that I am he which searcheth the reins and hearts: and I will give unto every one of you according to your works.

24   But unto you I say, and unto the rest in Thy-a-ti'ra, as many as have not this doctrine, and which have not known the depths of Satan, as they speak; I will put upon you none other burden.

25   But that which ye have *already* hold fast till I come.

26   And he that overcometh, and keepeth my works unto the end, to him will I give power over the nations:

27   And he shall rule them with a rod of iron; as the vessels of a potter shall they be broken to shivers: even as I received of my Father.

28   And I will give him the morning star.

29   He that hath an ear, let him hear what the Spirit saith unto the churches.

Chapter 2

Church at Ephesus, Pergamos, Thyatira

To each of the seven churches (plural) represents all churches in all ages and in all situations. These are things each Christian will face at some point in time. To each church Jesus reveals himself in one of the ways we see him in Revelation 1:12, 18. To Ephesus he is the one who holds the seven stars in his right hand. These stars represent the leader of each church: Also he is walking in the midst of the seven golden candlesticks. He is constantly watching each church. He knows all that goes on in every local church. All the good that we do can never offset the bad we do. We'll be held accountable unless we repent, which is commanded to five of the seven churches. This church was credited with many good qualities but they had fallen or gone back from their original position. The Lord could not accept this. How many churches have gone back and fallen from their original stand they took in the beginning and have never repented. This is why so many church doors are closed in America. The candlesticks or light in the community has been removed. Jesus said either make the tree good and its fruit good or make it bad and its fruit bad. We cannot have it both ways. If we do overcome we can eat of the tree of life or have eternal life. To Smyrna Jesus is the first and last which was dead and is alive. This church was facing great persecution to the point of death. So Jesus said I have been dead now I am alive. You don't have to fear death just be faithful until you die or are killed, then I will give you a crown of life. Notice Jesus did not tell this church you won't have to suffer but to be faithful in doing so. This is not what we want to hear today but if you have an ear you had better listen. Those that overcome will not be hurt by the second death. To Pergomas he is the one with the sharp two-edged sword. This church had good works. They had not denied the faith even when Antipas was martyred among them. But they had those that were teaching the doctrine at Balaam to defile themselves with eating things sacrificed to idols and also to commit fornication. Also, they had the doctrine of the Nicolaitanes. Jesus is revealing himself as the one with a sharp sword. Now he is ready to use it if they do not repent.

9

Repenting is not a one time thing. It is a regular part of the Christian life if we want to overcome. To this church if they did repent they could eat of the hidden manna (this was angel food from heaven) and also receive a white stone with a new name written in it. Jesus said he was the real bread from heaven. To most of the world Jesus is still the hidden manna. All through the scriptures we see people who get new names. This name will identify them with their position in Christ. To the church at Thyatira Jesus is the one with eyes like a flame of fire and feet like fine brass. This church had works, charity, service, faith and patience and their last work to be more than the first. But they suffered a woman with a Jezebel spirit to teach her theology. The word suffered means to permit or just leave alone. Most churches are very much like this. They permit or just leave alone some things or people in the church if it increases attendance or moneys brought in. But this will be found out even though a lot of good things are happening. The eyes of our Lord can see it all. Also, the feet of brass speaks of judgment and this will always happen to any church that allows this. God always gives space for repentance but if none comes, judgment will fall. He also will not allow children born into the church by spiritual fornication to remain. Jesus said, I search the reins and hearts of my people and will reward you according to your work. Jesus said unto you I say and unto the rest if you are not guilty of any of this I will not burden you. He is talking to the Shepard and the sheep. Keep a good testimony until I come. We must all overcome and keep our faith until the end. To those that do he will give authority over the nations to rule with a rod of iron. I will also give him the morning star, which is Jesus himself. (Revelation 22:16)

CHAPTER 3

AND unto the angel of the church in Sardis write; These things saith he that hath the seven Spirits of God, and the seven stars; I know thy works, that thou hast a name that thou livest, and art dead.

2   Be watchful, and strengthen the things which remain, that are ready to die: for I have not found thy works perfect before God.

3   Remember therefore how thou hast received and heard, and hold fast, and repent. If there fore thou shalt not watch, I will come on thee as a thief, and thou shalt not know what hour I will come upon thee.

4   Thou hast a few names even in Sardis which have not defiled their garments; and they shall walk with me in white: for they are worthy.

5   He that overcometh, the same shall be clothed in white raiment; and I will not blot out his name out of the book of life, but I will confess his name before my Father, and before his angels.

6   He that hath an ear, let him hear what the Spirit saith unto the churches.

7   And to the angel of the church in Philadelphia write; These things saith he that is holy, he that is true, he that hath the key of David, he that openeth, and no man shutteth; and shutteth, and no man openeth;

8   I know thy works: behold, I have set before thee an open door, and no man can shut it: for thou hast a little strength, and hast kept my word, and hast not denied my name.

9   Behold, I will make them of the synagogue of Satan, which say they are Jews, and are not, but do lie; behold, I will make them to come and worship before thy feet, and to know that I have loved thee.

10   Because thou hast kept the word of my patience, I also will keep thee from the hour of temptation, which shall come upon all the world, to try them that dwell upon the earth.

11   Behold, I come quickly: hold that fast which thou hast, that no man take thy crown.

12   Him that overcometh will I make a pillar in the temple of my God, and he shall go no more out: and I will write upon him the name of my God, and the name of the city of my God, *which* is new Jerusalem, which cometh down out of heaven from my God: and *I will write upon him* my new name.

13   He that hath an ear, let him hear what the Spirit saith unto the churches.

14 And unto the angel of the church of the La-od-i-ce'ans write; These things saith the Amen, the faithful and true witness, the beginning of the creation of God;

15 I know thy works, that thou art neither cold nor hot: I would thou wert cold or hot.

16 So then because thou art lukewarm, and neither cold nor hot, I will spue thee out of my mouth.

17 Because thou sayest, I am rich, and increased with goods, and have need of nothing; and knowest not that thou art wretched, and miserable, and poor, and blind, and naked:

18 I counsel thee to buy of me gold tried in the fire, that thou mayest be rich; and white raiment, that thou mayest be clothed, and that the shame of thy nakedness do not appear; and anoint thine eyes with eyesalve, that thou mayest see.

19 As many as I love, I rebuke and chasten: be zealous therefore, and repent.

20 Behold, I stand at the door, and knock: if any man hear my voice, and open the door, I will come in to him, and will sup with him, and he with me.

21 To him that overcometh will I grant to sit with me in my throne, even as I also overcame, and am set down with my Father in his throne.

22 He that hath an ear, let him hear what the Spirit saith unto the churches.

Chapter 3

Church at Sardis, Philadelphia, Laodicea

To Sardis, Jesus is saying I am the one with the seven spirits of God and also the seven stars. Jesus is saying everybody is congratulating you for your work but I know you are dead. He said be watchful and strengthen the things that remain that are ready to die. Your works are less than perfect. The only avenue of escape is to repent. If not I am coming like a thief and will catch you unprepared. There are a few in Sardis who have clean garments and to those will be given the privilege of walking with Christ. To those that overcome they will be clothed with white raiment and their name will remain in the book of life because Jesus will testify for them.

To the church at Philadelphia Jesus is the Holy and true one with the key of David. This is quoted in Isaiah 22:22, and the key of the house of David I will lay upon his shoulder so he shall open and none shall shut and he shall shut and none shall open. The name David means beloved. Jesus is saying those that I love I can keep because I have the key. I control everything. To this church Jesus has given an open door and no man can shut it. This very much applies to our time. Until God shuts the door it will stay open. But in this country of ours men are trying everywhere to shut the gospel doors. They have taken prayer out of almost all public places. Removed the Ten Commandments from public places and even now they are trying to silence the church. But this door will stay open until the Lord comes. When it is closed, men will cry to get in but will not be able. In Matthew 25 Jesus tells us about the end time he is talking about in the 24th chapter. Jesus is saying don't try to set a date for my return, just stay ready. But in these days we live in, most all Christians come to the conclusion time is at hand for Jesus' return. Although some are wise and some are foolish they all think the Lord has delayed his coming and are going to sleep.

Paul said in Hebrews 10:37 He that shall come will come and will not tarry. To the church it looks like he is tarrying but to Jesus he will be right on time. Jesus controls the door not the church. Notice also when the door is shut and those that were ready went in where they were secure. The foolish who were not ready think they have to just knock on the door. What does Jesus say? He answered them with an "I KNOW YOU NOT". No one will be left behind that was ready. Those that are not ready will never get in. When the door is shut it cannot be opened. It is over for the Gentiles. The next phrase has not come to pass, yet the Jews who were identified as the synagogue of Satan because of their blindness of the gospel and persecution of the church have earned this name. Before the church is gone the Jews will not only recognize the church will bow down and know just how much Jesus loves it. They will come to understand that Christ has already come and died for His Church. This church has kept the word with patience. They did not grow weary. The Lord said that he would keep them from the hour of temptation coming upon the earth. In Revelation 14:7, the angel is saying with a loud voice fear God and give glory to Him for the hour of His judgment is come and worship Him that made heaven and earth and the sea and the fountains of waters. This is just before the Lord comes back on a cloud in Revelation 14:14. This angel in verse 7 tells the world to repent and give God the glory for the hour of his judgment is come. This is what the Lord said he would keep this church from. Jesus said, behold I come quickly, keep yourself from evil. Stay as you are and you will receive a crown. Again we have to overcome no matter what it is. Revelation 21:7 He that overcometh shall inherit all things: and I'll be his God, and he shall be my son. Jesus said that he would make them a pillar in the temple of God. They would not go out but stay in the presence of God. No greater honor than this could ever be. They would receive the name of God written on them. And the name of the city of God; is New Jerusalem. Jesus also said I will write upon you my new name. Be a success for God and he will crown you with blessings overflowing. Listen to what the spirit is saying. To the Laodicea church Jesus is the amen, faithful and true witness, the beginning of the creation of God. He is saying this to a church that is dead and cold.

Amen in the Bible demonstrated excitement and conviction about God's promises. This church was just about the end of God's creation and surely they were not a true witness. Jesus always meets us where we are, showing us his best. This church has no good or bad works they were operating under the assumption that the best policy to serve God was don't get involved with the world; but to just make themselves a very nice nest. Jesus said you are not hot or cold. They were lukewarm. You have to be hot before becoming lukewarm, so at some point in time this church was on fire. Like most churches they were living in the past with their relationship with God, the old remember when. Ezekiel said to Israel, the righteousness of the righteous shall not deliver him in the day of his transgression 33:12. They were saying I am rich and increased with goods and have need for nothing. Most of the preaching today is centered round having abundance. Name it and claim it. Just sow a seed and reap a great harvest. We have mega churches where there are thousands of people, but very few people really know each other. They are good places to attend and still lose yourself. It is like the little one room schoolhouse where attention was personal. You know who needs help and in what areas and we produced enough people from them to make this a great country. But now all the little schools have been consolidated and we have lost a generation of children in doing so. When Jesus wanted to save the world he did not call five thousand or even five hundred. He chose twelve men and tutored them for three years. They turned the world upside down. Bigger is not always better. The mega churches are a splendor to look at with all the finest technology and conveniences. We try to do with money what the early church did with prayer. When was the last time you heard a preacher preach on I Timothy 6:10 but Godliness with contentment is a great gain. For we brought nothing into this world, and it is certain we can carry nothing out and having food and raiment let us be therewith content. But they that will be rich fall into temptation and a snare, and into many foolish and hurtful lusts, which drown men in destruction and perdition. For the love of money is the root of all evil: which while some coveted after they have erred from the faith, and pierced themselves through with many sorrows.

CHAPTER 4

AFTER this I looked, and, behold, a door *was* opened in heaven: and the first voice which I heard *was* as it were of a trumpet talking with me; which said, Come up hither, and I will shew thee things which must be hereafter.

2   And immediately I was in the spirit: and, behold, a throne was set in heaven, and *one* sat on the throne.

3   And he that sat was to look upon like a jasper and sardine stone: and *there was* a rainbow round about the throne, in sight like unto an emerald.

4   And round about the throne *were* four and twenty seats: and upon the seats I saw four and twenty elders sitting, clothed in white raiment; and they had on their heads crowns of gold.

5   And out of the throne proceeded lightnings and thunderings and voices: and *there were* seven lamps of fire burning before the throne, which are the seven Spirits of God.

6   And before the throne *there was* a sea of glass like unto crystal: and in the midst of the throne, and round about the throne, *were* four beasts full of eyes before and behind.

7   And the first beast *was* like a lion, and the second beast like a calf, and third beast had a face as a man, and the fourth beast *was* like a flying eagle.

8   And the four beasts had each of them six wings about *him*; and *they were* full of eyes within: and they rest not day and night, saying Holy, holy, holy, Lord God Almighty, which was, and is, and is to come.

9   And when those beasts give glory and honour and thanks to him that sat on the throne, who liveth for ever and ever,

10   The four and twenty elders fall down before him that sat on the throne, and worship him that liveth for ever and ever, and cast their crowns before the throne, saying,

11   Thou art worthy, O Lord, to receive glory and honour and power: for thou hast created all things, and for thy pleasure they are and were created.

Chapter 4

In the Presence of God

This door in heaven is going to open for John about three or four times as he begins to describe all that he is going to see. No where in the scriptures does it say that John represents the church. The voice like a trumpet speaks directly to John. He is the one receiving the revelation. John said immediately I was in the spirit. I do not believe that all the saints would go to heaven without some recognition of them in the scripture here.

In Revelation 14:14-16 gives us a picture of the rapture just as Christ said that he would. The throne of God was set and it could not be shaken or moved. Meaning there is no power to upset it. Psalm 45:6 Thy throne, oh God, is forever and ever. Also Psalm 103:19 The Lord hath prepared his throne in the heavens; and his kingdoms ruleth over all.

Notice the one sitting upon the throne was to be looked upon like a jasper stone. Note description given in Revelation 21:11 Having the glory of God: and her light was like unto a stone most precious, even like a jasper stone, clear as crystal. The stone is clear as crystal representing the purity of God and also the oneness of God. Not a shade of mixture is seen. The sardine stone, which is red in color, represents that our God is a consuming fire. Also, a rainbow around about the throne in sight like unto an emerald. One of God's favorite colors is green covering a large portion of the earth.

Round about the throne or circling the throne were twenty-four seats with twenty-four elders sitting on them in white raiment with a crown of gold on their heads. These twenty-four elders worship God because they are created beings. They do not represent the Old or New Testament saints. In Revelation 5:8 And when he had taken the book, the four beasts and four and twenty elders fell down before the Lamb, having everyone of them harps, and golden vials full of odors, which are the prayers of saints. They are Gods personal ministers. They are from one end to the other end of this book.

Notice when the great multitude appears in Revelation 7:9-11 they are there and Revelation 14:3 they are there and even in Revelation 19:1-4; And after these things I heard a great voice of much people in heaven, saying, Alleluia; Salvation, and glory, and honor, and power, unto the Lord our God: For true and righteous are his judgments: for he hath judged the great whore, which did corrupt the earth with her fornication, and hath avenged the blood of his servants at her hand. And again they said, Alleluia. And her smoke rose up for ever and ever. And the four and twenty elders and the four beasts fell down and worshipped God that sat on the throne, saying, Amen; Alleluia. They are still called the twenty-four elders. When John first entered heaven all he could see was God sitting on the throne in his brightness but as he stood there longer he begins to see more and more. There is lightning, thundering, voices, and seven lamps of fire representing the seven spirit of God. Heaven is a busy place. Now he sees a sea of glass like unto crystal before the throne. Notice this sea of glass before the throne is perfectly calm. No one in heaven is making any ripples in the rule of God. All is smooth as glass. Now he sees four beast or creatures before the throne full of eyes before and behind. John does not say they were but they were like unto. The third beast had a face as a man but he does not say it was a man's face. Each creature has six wings about him and they were full of eyes and continually day and night they are saying holy, holy, holy Lord God Almighty. He was, he is and he is to come. In heaven God is worshipped continually as he sits on his throne. Honor and thanks are given him by the four creatures. All honor in heaven and earth are to be given to God. Honor is recognition for some accomplishment and God is responsible for it all. Also thanks because he has made a way for all mankind to enjoy his heaven. Now the twenty-four elders fall down to worship him because God is forever and ever. They also cast their crown before him saying in verse 11 Thou art worthy, O Lord, to receive glory and honor and power: for thou hast created all things, and for thy pleasure they are and were created. We see this more clearly in Ephesians 1:9-14.

This is why God is to be continually worshipped.

CHAPTER 5

AND I saw in the right hand of him that sat on the throne a book written within and on the backside, sealed with seven seals.

2   And I saw a strong angel proclaiming with a loud voice, Who is worthy to open the book, and to loose the seals thereof?

3   And no man in heaven, nor in earth, neither under the earth, was able to open the book, neither to look thereon,

4   And I wept much, because no man was found worthy to open and to read the book, neither to look thereon.

5   And one of the elders saith unto me, Weep not: behold, the Lion of the tribe of Juda, the Root of David, hath prevailed to open the book, and to loose the seven seals thereof.

6   And I beheld, and, lo, in the midst of the throne and of the four beasts, and in the midst of the elders, stood a Lamb as it had been slain, having seven horns and seven eyes, which are the seven Spirits of God sent forth into all the earth.

7   And he came and took the book out of the right hand of him that sat upon the throne.

8   And when he had taken the book, the four beasts and four and twenty elders feel down before the Lamb, having every one of them harps, and golden vials full of odours, which are the prayers of saints.

9   And they sung a new song, saying, Thou art worthy to take the book, and to open the seals thereof: for thou wast slain, and hast redeemed us to God by thy blood out of every kindred, and tongue, and people, and nation;

10   And hast made us unto our God kings and priests: and we shall reign on the earth.

11   And I beheld, and I heard the voice of many angels round about the throne and the beasts and the elders: and the number of them was ten thousand times ten thousand, and thousands of thousands;

12   Saying with a loud voice, Worthy is the Lamb that was slain to receive power, and riches, and wisdom, and strength, and honour, and glory, and blessing.

13   And every creature which is in heaven, and on the earth, and under the earth, and such as are in the sea, and all that are in them, heard I saying, Blessing, and honour, and glory, and power, *be* unto him that sitteth upon the throne, and unto the Lamb for ever and ever.

14 And the four beasts said, Amen. And the four and twenty elders fell down and worshipped him that liveth for ever and ever.

Chapter 5

Christic and the Sealed Book

Now John can even see the Lamb of God and in his hand a book with seven seals upon it. In the book is contained the complete redemption of all mankind and also the total destruction of the devil and all evil. Remember that God has given all authority to his son that all men would worship the Son even as they do the Father. A great proclamation is made. Who is worthy to open the book? Immediately a search is made to find someone but no man is found worthy. Man does not control the destiny of things. The first man Adam has surrendered all to the devil so now it is up to God to provide a way and it was found in the second man Jesus Christ. He will never fail. John begins to weep because no one has been found worthy to open or even to look at the book. One of the elders told John not to weep because the Lion of the Tribe of Judea, the Root of David hath prevailed to open the book and break the seals. Here we begin to see Christ as the one he proclaimed to be. Revelation 1:8 I am Alpha and Omega, the beginning and the ending; saith the Lord, which is, and which was, and which is to come, the Almighty. This is the beginning of the end for the world. Sin and evil will now be exposed. The earth is going to experience the wrath of the Lamb. John has been in the presence of the throne of God for some time but he continues to see heaven unfold and more and more activity around it. He said, I looked and behold in the midst of the throne and of the four beasts and elder stood a Lamb as it had been slain. Now we see why Christ had to die. It was only through his death and resurrection that he is going to overcome. He has seven horns and seven eyes representing the seven spirits of God. The number seven signifies that he is complete power and wisdom. There is no one his equal. He came and took the book from him (God) that sat on the throne. God has given him all power and authority. All judgments are committed to the Son.

When he had taken the book, Heaven begins to rejoice. The four beasts and the twenty-four elder worship. Also they have golden vials full of odors. These are the prayers of the saints. Our prayers are all on record in Heaven. They never lose their power with God. What we commit to God he will use. 11 Timothy 1:12 For I know whom I have believed, and am persuaded that he is able to keep that which I have committed unto him against that day.

We find that from here until Chapter 16 that all things that will be going on will be seasoned with the prayers of the saints. The four beasts and twenty-four elder begin to sing a new song. The Lamb is worthy not only to open the book but to loose every seal because he was slain and by his death redemption through his blood. Because of this we will be unto God Kings and Priests and reign on the earth. Again John looks at the throne and now he sees angels all around. The number could be in the hundreds of millions. Heaven is a big place and all the angels are saying with a loud voice, worthy is the Lamb that was slain to receive power, riches, wisdom, strength, honor, glory and blessings. There are seven of these attributes crowning the Lamb in his perfection. Notice all creation in Heaven and earth and under the earth in the sea and everywhere are giving the same honor to the Father as well as to the Son. Heaven gives it a hardy Amen and they fall down and worship.

CHAPTER 6

AND I saw when the Lamb opened one of the seals, and I heard, as it were the noise of thunder, one of the four beasts saying, Come and see.

2   And I saw, and behold a white horse: and he that sat on him had a bow; and a crown was given unto him: and he went forth conquering, and to conquer.

3   And when he had opened the second seal, I heard the second beast say, Come and see.

4   And there went out another horse *that* was red: and *power* was given to him that sat thereon to take peace from the earth, and that they should kill one another: and there was given unto him a great sword.

5   And when he had opened the third seal, I heard the third beast say, Come and see. And I beheld, and lo a black horse; and he that sat on him had a pair of balances in his hand.

6   And I heard a voice in the midst of the four beasts say, A measure of wheat for a penny, and three measures of barley for a penny; and *see* thou hurt not the oil and the wine.

7   And when he had opened the fourth seal, I heard the voice of the fourth beast say, Come and see.

8   And I looked, and behold a pale horse: and his name that sat on him was Death, and Hell followed with him. And Power was given unto them over the fourth part of the earth, to kill with sword, and with hunger, and with death, and with the beasts of the earth.

9   And when he had opened the fifth seal, I saw under the altar the souls of them that were slain for the word of God, and for the testimony which they held:

10   And they cried with a loud voice, saying, How long, O Lord, holy and true, dost thou not judge and avenge our blood on them that dwell on the earth?

11   And white robes were given unto every one of them; and it was said unto them, that they should rest yet for a little season, until their fellowservants also and their brethren, that should be killed as they were, should be fulfilled.

12   And I beheld when he had opened the sixth seal, and, lo, there was a great earthquake; and the sun became black as sackcloth of hair, and the moon became as blood;

13   And the stars of heaven fell unto the earth, even as a fig tree casteth her untimely figs, when she is shaken of a mighty wind.

14   And the heaven departed as a scroll when it is rolled together; and every mountain and island were moved out of their places.

15   And the kings of the earth, and the great men, and the rich men, and the chief captains, and the mighty men, and every bondman, and every free man, hid themselves in the dens and in the rocks of the mountains;

16   And said to the mountains and rocks, Fall on us, and hide us from the face of him that sitteth on the throne, and from the wrath of the Lamb:

17   For the great day of his wrath is come; and who shall be able to stand?

Chapter 6

Opening of the Seals

Now the Lamb is beginning to open the seals. No one else in Heaven or earth or in the earth has the power to do this. This book is about the Lamb of God and the Revelation of him. He is going to be in complete control of all that take place in all the proceeding chapters of the book. Remember all power and all authority has been given to him. The crown in verse 2, the power in verse 4 and also the power in verse 8 are given to him. Everyone and everything will operate only in the limits of the Lamb. The first six seals give us a keyhole view from the rise of the Anti-Christ imitating the Lord as he rides out on a white horse until the great day of the wrath of the Lamb and the throne of God. Also, the complete and utter destruction of all evil. The first seal is broken and one of the four beasts proclaim to John to come and see. He said behold a white horse. The white horse represents the false purity and the power of the Anti Christ. White, being purity and the horse represents power just as horsepower represents the power of an engine. The one that is sitting on the horse has a bow. It does not say that he had any arrows but this man is going to be a deceiver. He is not Christ because Christ always has a sword in the scriptures. Notice a crown is given to him informing us that his authority is coming from another even though he is operating under the authority of Satan. Satan has to operate under the control of the Lord. Now he is going to go forth conquering and to conquer. All of this will be under the cover of deception until he has gotten complete control on the world. Then we will see just who this person is as Paul said in 11 Thessalonians 2:8

And then shall that Wicked be revealed, whom the Lord shall consume with the spirit of his mouth, and shall destroy with the brightness of his coming. This book and the seven seals represent to the world and Satan that God has given him the authority to execute all judgment over the world of evil and the power of Satan. Notice that God had the book but he has given it to the Lamb because he has the keys to death, hell and the grave. We could never praise the Lamb of God enough for defeating all our enemies and giving us the victory through him. As soon as the Anti Christ has conquered the world through deception he is now ready to declare war on mankind.

This horse is red, representing power and blood. Peace will be taken back because it was through peace that he deceived the world. Christ has promised us peace through his blood but men always want peace without God and there is none. After the false peace there is now going to be war. Men will kill and be killed. Jesus told us in John 8:44; ye are of your father the devil, and the lusts of your father ye will do. He was a murderer from the beginning, and abode not in the truth, because there is no truth in him. When he speaketh a lie, he speaketh of his own: for he is a liar, and the father of it. As the third seal is broken we see a black horse. Black represents the despair and bleakness of mankind after the war of seal two. Farms will not produce, and land will be destroyed with war machines and the ammunitions of war. There is always a great waste in battle. Food supplies will be going to the Army's. Food will be rationed to the point of just getting enough to eat. One meal will take a day's wages. Luxury items will still be available to those of the upper echelon. The fourth beast is saying, come and see. This horse is very pale, the rider upon this horse is death and of course hell is close by. After wars and famine, death is almost unavoidable. One fourth part of the earth will be killed by sword, hunger and with death. This could mean that plagues and diseases will be rampant. Men would also be killed by the beast of the earth. The fifth seal is opened without the usual come and see. John saw under the altar the souls that had been killed. These souls are on hold until more of their number will be added. These people were killed for the word of God and the testimony they held. All martyred saints will be here.

They were crying out for revenge on those that had killed them. They wanted their blood avenged by the Lord. They were given white robes and told to rest for a little while until their fellow servants and also their brethren that should be killed would arrive. This is speaking in positive terms. This will be fulfilled; meaning that there are people who will die before surrendering to Satan and the beast.

This group of people show up again in Revelation 20:4 And I saw thrones, and they sat upon them, and judgment was given unto them: and I saw the souls of them that were beheaded for the witness of Jesus, and for the word of God, and which had not worshipped the beast, neither his image, neither had received his mark upon their foreheads, or in their hands; and they lived and reigned with Christ a thousand years. Now we see who the fellow servants and brethren are, the people who did not worship the beast or his system, both Jew and Gentile, because their names were written in the book of life. Nowhere in the scriptures does it say there will be two folds. Listen to what Jesus said in John 10:16 and other sheep I have, which are not of this fold: them also I must bring, and they shall hear my voice; and there shall be one fold, and one shepherd. Also in Ephesians 2:14-18 For he is our peace, who hath made both one, and hath broken down the middle wall or partition between us; Having abolished in his flesh the enmity, even the law of commandments contained in ordinances; for to make in himself of twain one new man, so making peace; And that he might reconcile both unto God in one body by the cross, having slain the enmity thereby: And came and preached peace to you which were afar off, and to them that were nigh. For through him we both have access by one Spirit unto the Father. In Revelation 13:8; And all that dwell upon the earth shall worship him, whose names are not written in the book of life of the Lamb slain from the foundation of the world. This is said in the present tense. These are the only two classes of people, those that have their name in the book and those that worship the beast.

There will be two resurrections. One at the end of the tribulation and then one at the end of the Millennial reign. Those in the first are the martyrs and the tribulation saints. They will rule with Christ during the Millennium. Notice what Paul said in Hebrews 11:35; women received their dead raised to life again: and others were tortured, not accepting deliverance; that they might obtain a better resurrection. There are people who do not love their life more than the Lord. Revelation 12:11; and they overcame him by the blood of the Lamb and by the word of their testimony; and they loved not their lives unto the death. The better resurrection is for those who gave all, not accepting deliverance. All that enter the tribulation period will rule with Christ in the Millennium. The Laodicea church was given this hope. Revelation 3:21 To him that overcometh will I grant to sit with me in my throne, even as I also overcame, and am set down with my Father in his throne. These will sit with Christ in his throne. Notice what Paul said in 1 Thessalonians 4:13-18 But I would not have you to be ignorant, brethren, concerning them which are asleep, that ye sorrow not, even as others which have no hope. For if we believe that Jesus died and rose again, even so them also which sleep in Jesus will God bring with him. Some people die with no hope. They are lost. But Paul said if we believe that Jesus died and rose for us when we die God will bring those people back with him. God does not come to the earth until after the Millennium to sit at the great white throne judgment. From verse 15 on he is saying those that enter the tribulation period will be caught up to meet the Lord in the air. This group is separate from those that come back with God in verse 14. Those that remain from the start of the tribulation who die a martyr's death and those that remain will be raptured up to meet the Lord in the air and will reign with Christ for the thousand years. These are those in Revelation 6:9-11 and also the same group of people in Revelation 20:4. This will be the first resurrection. God reserved the right to do what he chooses with his own. Notice what the Lord said in Matthew 19:29-30; and everyone that hath forsaken houses, or brethren, or sisters, or father, or mother, or wife, or children, or lands, for my name's sake, shall receive a hundredfold, and shall inherit everlasting life. (Emphasis is on eternal life) But many that are first shall be last; and the last shall be first. Notice many that are first shall be last and the last shall be first. This is concerning the resurrection. All will have eternal life but in God's order. Notice what they said about those that came in at the eleventh hour in Matthew 20. They were upset and complained to the Lord of the vineyard because they were paid first. This is what Jesus said to those that complained, Verses 14-16 Take that thine is, and go thy way: I will give unto this last, even as unto thee. Is it not lawful for me to do what I will with mine own? Is thine eye evil, because I am good? So the last shall be first, and the first last; for many are called, but few chosen. In verse 12-17 we see the end. God's wrath is being poured out just as described in the seventh vial. Note the similarity, first a great earthquake, Jerusalem is divided into three parts. This could correspond to Zechariah 13:8-9; and it shall come to pass, that in all the land, saith the Lord, two parts therein shall be cut off and die: but the third shall be left therein. And I will bring the third part through the fire, and will refine them as silver is refined, and will try them as gold is tried: they shall call on my name, and I will hear them: I will say, It is my people: and they shall say The LORD is my God.

The Sequence of Events in Revelation 6:12-17
1. A Great Earthquake
2. Sun Became Black as Sackcloth
3. Moon Became Blood
4. Stars of Heaven Fall
5. Heaven Departs and Rolled Away
6. Every Mountain and Island Moved Out of Place
7. All Men Hide In The Earth and Cry For It To Fall In On Them
8. The Great Judgment

The Sequence of Events in Revelation 16:17-21
1. A Great Earthquake, A Mighty Earthquake
2. The Great City Divided
3. The Cities of the Nations Fall
4. Gods Wrath on Babylon.
5. Every Island Fled Away
6. The Mountains Were Not Found
7. Men Are Bombarded With Great Hail Stones
8. They Blaspheme God

Sequence of Events in Acts 2:19-20
1. Signs and Wonders in Heaven
2. Signs in the Earth, Blood, Fire and Vapor of Smoke
3. Sun to Turn Dark or Black
4. Moon Into Blood
5. Then the Lord's Return

The great question is who will stand? Are you going to be ready? In 1 Corinthians 10:12 Paul said, wherefore let him that thinketh he standeth take heed lest he fall. Also in Hebrews 10:31 he said It's a fearful thing to fall into the hands of the living God. All who want to stand for the Lord can do so if they wish. In 2 Peter 1:4-10; whereby are given unto us exceeding great and precious promises: that by these ye might be partakers of the divine nature, having escaped the corruption that is in the world through lust. And besides this, giving all diligence, add to your faith virtue; and to virtue knowledge; and to knowledge temperance; and to temperance patience; and to patience godliness; 'And to godliness brotherly kindness; and to brotherly kindness charity. For if these things be in you, and abound, they make you that ye shall neither be barren nor unfruitful in the knowledge of our Lord Jesus Christ. But he that lacketh these things is blind, and cannot see afar off, and hath forgotten that he was purged from his old sins. Wherefore the rather, brethren, give diligence to make your calling and election sure: for if ye do these things, ye shall never fall. You see there is a way to stand and never fall.

CHAPTER 7

AND after these things I saw four angels standing on the four corners of the earth, holding the four winds of the earth, that the wind should not blow on the earth, nor on the sea, nor on any tree.

2   And I saw another angel ascending from the east, having the seal of the living God: and he cried with a loud voice to the four angels, to whom it was given to hurt the earth and the sea,

3   Saying, Hurt not the earth, neither the sea, nor the trees, till we have sealed the servants of our God in their foreheads.

4   And I heard the number of them which were sealed: and *there were* sealed an hundred and forty *and* four thousand of all the tribes of the children of Israel.

5   Of the tribe of Juda *were* sealed twelve thousand. Of the tribe of Reuben were sealed twelve thousand. Of the tribe of Gad *were* sealed twelve thousand.

6   Of the tribe of A'ser *were* sealed twelve thousand. Of the tribe of Neph'tha-lim *were* sealed twelve thousand. Of the tribe of Ma-nas'ses *were* sealed twelve thousand.

7   Of the tribe of Simeon *were* sealed twelve thousand. Of the tribe of Levi *were* sealed twelve thousand. Of the tribe of Is'sa-char *were* sealed twelve thousand.

8   Of the tribe of Zab'u-lon *were* sealed twelve thousand. Of the tribe of Joseph *were* sealed twelve thousand. Of the tribe of Benjamin *were* sealed twelve thousand.

9   After this I beheld, and, lo, a great multitude, which no man could number, of all nations, and kindreds, and people, and tongues, stood before the throne, and before the Lamb, clothed with white robes, and palms in their hands;

10   And cried with a loud voice, saying, Salvation to our God which sitteth upon the throne, and unto the Lamb.

11   And all the angels stood round about the throne, and about the elders and the four beasts, and fell before the throne on their faces, and worshipped God.

12   Saying, Amen: Blessing, and glory, and wisdom, and thanksgiving, and honour, and power, and might, *be* unto our God for ever and ever. Amen

13   And one of the elders answered, saying unto me, What are these which are arrayed in white robes? and whence came they?

14   And I said unto him, Sir, thou knowest. And he said to me, These are they which came out of great tribulation, and have washed their robes, and made them white in the blood of the Lamb.

15   Therefore are they before the throne of God, and serve him day and night in his temple: and he that sitteth on the throne shall dwell among them.

16   They shall hunger no more, neither thirst any more; neither shall the sun light on them, nor any heat.

17   For the Lamb which is in the midst of the throne shall feed them ,and shall lead them into living fountains of waters: and God shall wipe away all tears from their eyes.

Chapter 7

144,000 Sealed the Great Multitude

In Chapter 7 verse I John sees four angels standing on the four corners of the earth holding the four winds North South East and West so they could not blow on the earth or sea nor any tree. Satan is the prince of the power of the air Ephesians 2:2 Satan also operates in the dimension between heaven and earth. So what God is getting ready to do he does not want any interference.

Another angel is now ascending from the East. This is where God's glory comes from. Ezekiel 43:2; and, behold, the glory of the God of Israel came from the way of the east: and his voice was like a noise of many waters: and the earth shined with his glory. These four angels are going to bring in the first four trumpets affecting the earth in Chapter 8. They have been commanded not do so until God had sealed his servants in their foreheads.

The number to be sealed is 144,000. Of all the tribes of Israel, Judah, Reuben, Gad, Aser, Nepthalim, Manasses, Simeon, Levi, Issachar, Zebulon, Joseph, Benjamin there would be 12,000 sealed from each. This seal is God's guarantee that this 144,000 will make it through. They are sealed here and Revelation 14:1 And I looked, and lo, a Lamb stood on the mount Zion; and with him an hundred forty and four thousand having his Father's name written in their foreheads. There are still 144,000 and not one is lost; When God does something it is Jew first then Gentile. Romans 2:11; for there is no respect of persons with God. It is Jew first but what he will do for the Jew he will do for the Gentile. In Romans 8:23 And not only they, but ourselves also, which have the first fruits of the Spirit, even we ourselves groan within ourselves, waiting for the adoption, to wit, the redemption of our body. They were the first fruits.

Now John sees a great multitude that no man could number. They were from all nations, all kindred, peoples and tongues. John wants us to know that from every point on the globe people will go to heaven.

They are standing before the throne and before the Lamb clothed in white robes and palms in their hand. Palms were used on the booths made for the feast of Tabernacle. Leviticus 23:40 Also in John 12:13 Took branches of palm trees, and went forth to meet him, and cried, Hosanna: Blessed is the King of Israel that cometh in the name of the Lord. The palms were a type of rejoicing before God. They give glory to God and the Lamb by crying "Salvation to our God". It is the gift of God to his people. Salvation is the great word in the scriptures gathering to itself justification, propitiation, grace, redemption, sanctification, imputation, forgiveness, and glorification. Salvation is God's package gift to mankind so he could be complete.

All the angels are standing around the throne. Jesus said that there would be joy in Heaven where one sinner repented. How much more over a multitude this big? The angels, the elders and the four beasts fall on their face and worship God. They are saying Amen (Let it be so). Blessings, glory, wisdom, thanksgiving, honor, power and might be to our God forever and forever Amen. There are usually always seven of these attributes given to God. One of the twenty-four elder approached John to ask him if he knew this great multitude. John replied I am sure that you know who they are and where they came from. The elder said to John, These are people who have come out of the great tribulation. God has guaranteed that 144,000 Jews would be sealed. So here God is saying look how many I am going to save of the Gentiles. The elder said to John, this great multitude are they which came out of this world. (Come is in the past tense, meaning they have already come out.) They did not go through the tribulation. They have washed their robes in the blood of the Lamb. Notice they are before the throne of God and serve him day and night in his temple, meaning they'll be before God's throne during the Millennium after this time there'll be no more days or nights and God will dwell among them. The elder said they shall hunger or thirst no more. This does not mean that they would never want food or water but that the Lamb would keep them satisfied forever. He continues to feed and give them water to drink. Remember Jesus is the bread of life and also the living water. Also notice what is said. The sun would not shine on them or any heat. This is the same group that Paul is talking about in I Thessalonians 4:14 For if we believe that Jesus died and rose again, even so them also which sleep in Jesus will God bring with him. Jesus is going to rule from Jerusalem for the thousand years. God himself does not come to earth until the thousand years are up. When God appears it is at the Great White throne. Time is no more. Notice also what is said, the sun would not shine on them or any heat. When Jesus is ruling from Jerusalem it will be measured by days, months and years. The sun will be shining all this time but this group will not be in it. The Lamb shall feed them and also lead them to living fountains of water. This water will flow from the throne of God. Revelation 22:1 And he shewed me a pure river of water of life, clear as crystal, proceeding out of the throne of God and of the Lamb. No more crying, every eye will be dry.

CHAPTER 8

AND when he had opened the seventh seal, there was silence in heaven about the space of half an hour.

2 And I saw the seven angels which stood before God; and to them were given seven trumpets.

3 And another angel came and stood at the altar, having a golden censer; and there was given unto him much incense, that he should offer *it* with the prayers of all saints upon the golden altar which was before the throne.

4 And the smoke of the incense, *which came* with the prayers of the saints, ascended up before God out of the angel's hand.

5 And the angel took the censer, and filled it with fire of the altar, and cast *it* into the earth: and there were voices, and thunderings, and lightnings, and an earthquake.

6. And the seven angels which had the seven trumpets prepared themselves to sound.

7 The first angel sounded, and there followed hail and fire mingled with blood, and they were cast upon the earth: and the third part of trees was burnt up, and all green grass was burnt up.

8 And the second angel sounded, and as it were a great mountain burning with fire was cast into the sea: and the third part of the sea became blood;

9 And the third part of the creatures which were in the sea, and had life, died; and the third part of the ships were destroyed.

10 And the third angel sounded, and there fell a great star from heaven, burning as it were a lamp, and it fell upon the third part of the rivers, and upon the fountains of waters;

11 And the name of the star is called Wormwood: and the third part of the waters became wormwood; and many men died of the waters, because they were made bitter.

12 And the fourth angel sounded, and the third part of the sun was smitten, and the third part of the moon, and the third part of the stars; so as the third part of them was darkened, and the day shone not for a third part of it, and the night likewise.

13 And I beheld, and heard an angel flying through the midst of heaven, saying with a loud voice, Woe, woe, woe, to the inhabiters of the earth by reason of the other voices of the trumpet of the three angels, which are yet to sound!

Chapter 8

The Seven Trumpets 1-4

So far six of the seven seals have been opened. These six seals just gave us a brief glimpse of what is to come. Six is the number of man. He was created on the sixth day.

Now the seventh seal is about to be opened. Seven the number of completion on the seventh day God rested. His labor was complete. Seven days make a complete week. There were seven lamps, seven churches, seven spirits of God. The number goes on. But this is the seventh seal and out of it will come the seven trumpets. No judgment from this seal but a revelation of things yet to come. When this seal is broken there is silence in Heaven for about half an hour. The only recorded time there is silence in Heaven. But now judgment will begin to fall upon the earth. The seals were open just to reveal. Now the trumpets will sound to proclaim the judgments of God. The seven angels are standing before God and they each receive a trumpet. Another angel came and stood at the altar. Now all those souls that were crying out for revenge can now see God begin his judgment on earth. This angel has a golden censer. Also he is given much incense in this censer. The incense in this censer will make a very delightful smell. But notice also the prayers of all saints and the word all saints. All prayers that make it to heaven are kept on file for future use. Prayers are out most important weapon. This incense with the prayer will ascend up to God. God's throne is high above all else in heaven. When these prayers come into contact with the incense they must have started smoking. Now that the censer is empty again, the angel fills it with fire from the altar and cast it upon the earth. There is great commotion on earth now. Voices, thundering, lightening, earthquakes, and the seven angels are already to sound.

When the trumpets begins to sound only a third part are affected. These trumpets are seasoned with mercy because of the prayer's of the saints. God is not trying to get even; he is trying to get the attention of people on earth. At the sound of the first trumpet hail and fire mingled with blood were cast upon the earth. In Exodus 9:22-25 And the Lord said unto Moses, Stretch forth thine hand toward heaven, that there may be hail in all the land of Egypt, upon man, and upon beast, and upon every herb of the field, throughout the land of Egypt. And Moses stretched forth his rod toward heaven: and the Lord sent thunder and hail, and the fire ran along upon the ground; and the Lord rained hail upon the land of Egypt. So there was hail, and fire mingled with the hail, very grievous, such as there was none like it in all the land of Egypt since it became a nation. And the hail smote throughout all the land of Egypt all that was in the field, both man and beast; and the hail smote every herb of the field, and breaks every tree of the field. This gives us an idea what it was like only there is blood with this. So much blood has been shed just in the last one hundred years. It is hard to estimate the quantity of blood that has been spilled. Even now there is little regard for human life.

A third part of the trees was burnt up and all green grass. Notice no loss of life. These are just warning shots. The second trumpet sounds. We don't know how much time there is between each trumpet but it will not just be one after the other. Trumpets have a better part of three years to happen in. A great mountain burning with fire is cast into the sea. This is probably the Mediterranean Sea. It is one of the biggest bodies of water in that area. The sea became blood. This is not a mountain of fire but as it were a mountain of fire. However, this could have been a mountain of blood. A third part of sea life dies also. A third part of ships were destroyed. Again there is no mention of human life. Although there could be with those ships destroyed. Again it is only a third part. Now it is time for the third angel to sound. As he does so there fell a great star from Heaven burning as it were a lamp. This star is producing a lot of light. It falls upon one third-part of rivers and upon the fountains of water. This means that the rivers were polluted and also the source of these waters. The waters continued to produce wormwood. Wormwood is a very bitter plant usually associated with a very sad or bitter experience. The waters were so bad that many men die from trying to drink it. Now we see the definite loss of life.

There is one more trumpet to sound in regards to what is said in verse 3 of Revelation 7. Saying, Hurt not the earth, neither the sea, nor the trees, till we have sealed the servants of our God on their foreheads. These plagues were designed to hurt the earth, the seas and trees, more than man. God is showing mercy to an undeserving world. A third part of the sun is smitten. A third part of the moon and also a third part of the stars are as well. This decreases light of each one by one third.

If the first three plagues were just in the area of the Mediterranean Sea, the fourth one can be seen worldwide. Most of Israel's enemies, though the world hates them, are scattered around the Mediterranean Sea area. God is going to bring the Jewish nation to repentance and also to bring judgment on the rest of the world. Now the next two trumpets will be more on humanity than nature. God is increasing the pressure on people for repentance.

CHAPTER 9

AND the fifth angel sounded, and I saw a star fall from heaven unto the earth: and to him was given the key of the bottomless pit.

2 And he opened the bottomless pit; and there arose a smoke out of the pit, as the smoke of a great furnace; and the sun and the air were darkened by reason of the smoke of the pit.

3 And there came out of the smoke locusts upon the earth: and unto them was given power, as the scorpions of the earth have power.

4 And it was commanded them that they should not hurt the grass of the earth, neither any green thing, neither any tree; but only those men which have not the seal of God in their foreheads.

5 And to them it was given that they should not kill them, but that they should be tormented five months: and their torment was as the torment of a scorpion, when he striketh a man.

6 And in those days shall men seek death, and shall not find it; and shall desire to die, and death shall flee from them.

7 And the shapes of the locusts were like unto horses prepared unto battle; and on their heads *were* as it were crowns like gold, and their faces *were* as the faces of men.

8 And they had hair as the hair of women, and their teeth were as *the teeth* of lions.

9 And they had breastplates, as it were breastplates of iron; and the sound of their wings was as the sound of chariots of many horses running to battle.

10 And they had tails like unto scorpions, and there were stings in their tails: and their power *was* to hurt men five months.

11 And they had a king over them, *which* is the angel of the bottomless pit, whose name in the Hebrew tongue is A-bad'don, but in the Greek tongue hath his name A-pol'ly-on.

12 One woe is past; *and*, behold, there come two woes more hereafter.

13 And the sixth angel sounded, and I heard a voice from the four horns of the golden altar which is before God,

14 Saying to the sixth angel which had the trumpet, Loose the four angels which are bound in the great river Euphra'tes.

15 And the four angels were loosed, which were prepared for an hour, and a day, and a month, and a year, for to slay the third part of men.

16 And the number of the army of the horsemen were two hundred thousand thousand: and I heard the number of them.

17 And thus I saw the horses in the vision, and them that sat on them, having breastplates of fire, and of jacinth, and brimstone: and the heads of the horses *were* as the heads of lions; and out of their mouths issued fire and smoke and brimstone.

18 By these three was the third part of men killed, by the fire, and by the smoke, and by the brimstone, which issued out of their mouths.

19 For their power is in their mouth, and in their tails: for their tails were like unto serpents, and had heads, and with them they do hurt.

20 And the rest of the men which were not killed by these plagues yet repented not of the works of their hands, that they should not worship devils, and idols of gold, and silver, and brass, and stone, and of wood: which neither can see, nor hear, nor walk:

21 Neither repented they of their murders, nor of their sorceries, nor of their fornication, nor of their thefts.

Chapter 9

The Seven Trumpets 5-6

We see a star fall from Heaven. This star could be a fallen angel; he came from Heaven with the key to the bottomless pit. But this also is a part of God's plan as we shall see. This pit has to be opened to let the beast out as told in Revelation 11:7 and when they shall have finished their testimony, the beast that ascendeth out of the bottomless pit shall make war against them, and shall overcome them, and kill them. Although he is not the one we are interested in now he soon will be. As the pit is opened a great cloud of smoke fills the sky so that the sun is darkened by it. Out of the smoke came locust with the power of scorpions. Now we see that the grass, trees or any green thing is not to be eaten by these creatures. They have only one mission. It is to go to those men who do not have the seal of God in their foreheads. Remember the ones that were sealed were of the tribes of Israel. These that were not sealed are those that did not meet God's standard of living. Those that are sealed had not defiled themselves. Revelation 14:4-5 these are they which were not defiled with women; for they are virgins. These are they which follow the Lamb whithersoever he goeth. These were redeemed from among men, being the first fruits unto God and to the Lamb, And in their mouth was found no guile: for they are without fault before the throne of God. Notice God does not want to kill them but to torment them for five months. They may desire to die and look for death but it will flee from them. The locust is a type of grasshopper, if you look at the head of one it looks very much like the head of a horse. On the crown of their head it was yellow; their face had the appearance of a man. They must have been very hairy. Their teeth were very strong and their body was very hard. As they went in great numbers they made very much noise. It was their tail that did the damage. In it was a stinger that injected poison. These creatures were to stay around for five months. If you read Joel Chapter 2: 1-18 Blow ye the trumpet in Zion and sound an alarm in my holy mountain: let all the inhabitants of the land tremble: for the day of the Lord cometh, for it is nigh at hand; A day of darkness and of gloominess, a day of clouds and of thick

43

darkness, as the morning spread upon the mountains: a great people and a strong; there hath not been ever the like, neither shall be any more after it, even to the years of many generations. A fire devoureth before them; and behind them a flame burneth: the land is as the Garden of Eden before them, and behind them a desolate wilderness; yea, and nothing shall escape them. The appearance of them is as the appearance of horses; and as horsemen, so shall they run. Like the noise of chariots on the tops of mountains shall they leap, like the noise of a flame of fire that devoureth the stubble, as a strong people set in battle array. Before their face the people shall be much pained: all faces shall gather blackness. They shall run like mighty men; they shall climb the wall like men of war; and they shall march everyone on his ways, and they shall not break their ranks: Neither shall one thrust another; they shall walk everyone in his path: and when they fall upon the sword, they shall not be wounded. They shall run to and fro in the city; they shall run upon the wall, they shall climb up upon the houses; they shall enter in at the windows like a thief. The earth shall quake before them; the heavens shall tremble: the sun and the moon shall be dark, and the stars shall withdraw their shining: And the Lord shall utter his voice before his army: for his camp is very great: for he is strong that executeth his word: for the day of the Lord is great and very terrible; and who can abide it? Therefore also now, saith the Lord, turn ye even to me with all your heart, and with fasting, and with mourning: And rend your heart, and not your garments, and turn unto the Lord your God: for he is gracious and merciful, slow to anger, and of great kindness, and repenteth him of the evil. Who knoweth if he will return and repent, and leave a blessing behind him; even a meat-offering and a drink-offering unto the Lord your God? Blow the trumpet in Zion, sanctify a fast, and call a solemn assembly: Gather the people, sanctify the congregation, assemble the elders, gather the children, and those that suck the breasts: let the bridegroom go forth of his chamber, and the bride out of her closet. Let the priests, the ministers of the Lord, weep between the porch and the altar, and let them say, Spare thy people, O Lord, and give not thine heritage to reproach, that the heathen should rule over them: wherefore should they say among the people, Where is their God? Then will the Lord be jealous for his land, and pity his people. By these scriptures you can see that God is getting his people ready to begin to seek Him. They have a King over them, the angel of the bottomless pit. His name is Abaddon, in Hebrew but in Greek it is Apollyon. Both names mean destroyer. This is the first of three woes that are to come. All three woes are related to the Jewish nation, as we shall see. Now comes the sixth trumpet. When it sounds a voice comes from the golden altar, which is before God saying to the angel, loose the four angels, which are bound in the Euphrates River. This river is in the sixth trumpet and also the sixth vial. This river is also mentioned in the Garden of Eden. It has played a vital role all through the scriptures. This river is going to be the boundary for the Jewish nation on the east side. Genesis 15:18 In the same day the Lord made a covenant with Abram, saying, Unto thy seed have I given this land, from the river of Egypt unto the great river, the river Euphrates. These four angels were bound and put in this river at some point in time but we have no indication when this took place. When they are released it is for the sole purpose of slaying one-third part of men. This could be worldwide or it could be the nations situated around the Mediterranean Sea. This will take place at exactly a date predetermined by God right down to the very hour of the day or night, month and year in the future. The four angels will control an army of 200,000,000 horsemen having breastplates of fire and jacinth and also brimstone. These breastplates were of fire. When fire is put to brimstone or sulfur, it burns with a blue flame, the color of jacinth. Very possibly these creatures were from hell since they were wearing breastplates of fire.

The head of these horses were as the heads of lions. Meaning that they were very fierce looking. Also from their mouth came fire, smoke and brimstone or burning sulfur. Maybe God is letting the earth see just what it is like in the lake of fire. Men were killed by what issued out of the mouth of these horses but also they had tails like serpents with heads that caused people much pain. The people on earth are in a blind rage against God. They will not repent of the works of their hands or of their murders, sorceries, fornication or their thefts. Repentance seems to be out of the question.

CHAPTER 10

AND I saw another mighty angel come down from heaven, clothed with a could: and a rainbow *was* upon his head, and his face *was* as it were the sun, and his feet as pillars of fire:

2   And he had in his hand a little book open: and he set his right foot upon the sea, and *his* left *foot* on the earth,

3   And cried with a loud voice, as *when* a lion roareth: and when he had cried, seven thunders uttered their voices.

4   And when the seven thunders had uttered their voices, I was about to write: and I heard a voice from heaven saying unto me, Seal up those things which the seven thunders uttered, and write them not.

5   And the angel which I saw stand upon the sea and upon the earth lifted up his hand to heaven,

6   And sware by him that liveth for ever and ever, who created heaven, and the things that therein are, and the earth, and the things that therein are, and the sea, and the things which are therein, that there should be time no longer:

7   But in the days of the voice of the seventh angel, when he shall begin to sound, the mystery of God should be finished, as he hath declared to his servants the prophets.

8   And the voice which I heard from heaven spake unto me again, and said, Go *and* take the little book which is open in the hand of the angel which standeth upon the sea and upon the earth.

9   And I went unto the angel, and said unto him, Give me the little book. And he said unto me, Take *it*, and eat it up; and it shall make thy belly bitter, but it shall be in thy mouth sweet as honey.

10   And I took the little book out of the angel's hand, and ate it up; and it was in my mouth sweet as honey: and as soon as I had eaten it, my belly was bitter.

11   And he said unto me, Thou must prophesy again before many peoples, and nations, and tongues, and kings.

Chapter 10

The Mighty Angel and the Little Book

This angel John sees here could very possibly be the Lamb that took the book from the hand of God. His dress corresponds to Jesus in Revelation Chapter 1.

Now the book is opened and all the seals have been broken. The next trumpet marks the beginning of the end. This angel is called a mighty angel. He is able to put one foot on land and the other on the sea. As he does so he cried with a loud voice like a roaring lion. It may be a cry of victory. When he had cried seven thunders uttered their voices. Usually when God speaks it is a sound like thunder but what is said is not to be recorded. John is told to seal up what is said. Although this is a book revealing things to come there are some things we do not need to know. So here are seven thunders that could reveal a lot of information but it is sealed up. We still have to live by faith. The angel now lifted up his hand to heaven and sware by the one who had created everything from Heaven to earth and the sea that there should be no more delay of time. Now listen to what he said in the days of the seventh angel when he begins to sound. The mystery of God should be finished as he has declared to his servants the prophets. Hear what Paul said about this mystery in Ephesians 1:9 having made known unto us the mystery of his will, according to his good pleasure which he hath purposed in himself. In Ephesians 3:1-10 For this cause I Paul, the prisoner of Jesus Christ for you Gentiles, If ye have heard of the dispensation of the grace of God which is given me to you-ward: How that by revelation he made known unto me the mystery; (as I wrote afore in few words, Whereby, when ye read, ye may understand my knowledge in the mystery of Christ) Which in other ages was not made known unto the sons of men, as it is now revealed unto his holy apostles and prophets by the Spirit; That the Gentiles should be fellow heirs, and of the same body, and partakers of his promise in Christ by the gospel: Whereof I was made a minister according to the gift of the grace of God given unto me by the effectual working of his power. Unto me, who am less than the least of all saints, is this grace given, that I should preach among the

Gentiles the un-searchable riches of Christ; And to make all men see what is the fellowship of the mystery, which from the beginning of the world hath been hid in God, who created all things by Jesus Christ: To the intent that now unto the principalities and powers in heavenly places might be known by the church the manifold wisdom of God. Now we see just what the angel is talking about. It is the church. It did not go in Chapter 4 of Revelation. Again in Romans Chapter 16:25-26 Now to him that is of power to establish you according to my gospel, and the preaching of Jesus Christ, according to the revelation of the mystery, which was kept secret since the world began, but now is made manifest, and by the scriptures of the prophets, according to the commandment of the everlasting God, made known to all nations for the obedience of faith. We see the revelation of the mystery again. In Ephesians 6:19-20 Paul speaks of this mystery again. He says it is the mystery of the gospel or the good news that God was going to create a church consisting of both Jew and Gentile. In Revelation 10:7 this mystery will be complete or finished. This will happen in the days (plural) when the seventh angel will begin to sound. The sixth trumpet has just sounded and this information is put in to prepare us for the days following the seventh trumpet. When the seventh angel does sound, it said the nations were angry and the wrath of God is getting ready to come. Also, time for the dead to be judged and rewards given to His servants, prophets, saints and all that fear the name of God. And to destroy those that were destroying the world. All this takes place between the last trumpet and the first vial at the wrath of God. In 1 Corinthians 15:51-52 Behold, I shew you a mystery; we shall not all sleep, but we shall all be changed, in a moment, in the twinkling of an eye at the last trump: for the trumpet shall sound, and the dead shall be raised incorruptible, and we shall be changed. Notice that Paul said at the last trump was when these things were going to happen. The dead raised and the living changed. Between the seventh trumpet and the first vial will be the rapture of the church as told in Revelation 14:14-15. I believe that the church will do great exploits when it is put to the test. All God is trying to do in this book is to get the people of the world to repent. All these plagues he brings upon the earth are not being put on the Christians. When God delivered the Hebrews from Pharaoh he made a distinction between Hebrew and Egyptian. Our enemy is the devil and God is our redeemer. Again a voice speaks to John saying take the little book, which is opened in the hand of the angel. John does as he is instructed. He is told that the book will be as sweet as honey in his mouth but very bitter in the stomach. It is like the parable of the sower when seeds fall on stony ground. Hear what Jesus said in Matthew 13:20-21 But he that received the seed into stony places, the same is he that heareth the word, and anon with joy receiveth it; Yet hath he not root in himself, but dureth for a while: for when tribulation or persecution ariseth because of the word, by and by he is offended. It is not always easy to digest the word of God but we have to take the bitter with the sweet. John is told that he must prophesy again before many peoples, nations, tongues and Kings. This prophecy of John, which Jesus gave him, has gone around the world to all nations in the last two thousand years, so John had a great audience. Other scripture references in respect to Revelation 10:7 include Colossians 1:24-27 Who now rejoice in my sufferings for you, and fill up that which is behind of the afflictions of Christ in my flesh for his body's sake, which is the church: Whereof I am made a minister, according to the dispensation of God which is given to me for you, to fulfill the word of God. Even the mystery which hath been hid from ages and from generations, but now is made manifest to his saints: To whom God would make known what is the riches of the glory of this mystery among the Gentiles; which is Christ in you, the hope of glory. Colossians 2:1-3 For I would that ye knew what great conflict I have for you, and for them at Laodicea, and for as many as have not seen my face in the flesh; That their hearts might be comforted, being knit together in love, and unto all riches of the full assurance of understanding, to the acknowledgement of the mystery of God, and of the Father, and of Christ in whom are hid all the treasures of wisdom and knowledge.

CHAPTER 11

AND there was given me a reed like unto a rod: and the angel stood, saying, Rise, and measure the temple of God, and the altar, and them that worship therein.

2   But the court which is without measure it not; for it is given unto the Gentiles: and the holy city shall they tread under foot forty *and* two months.

3   And I will give *power* unto my two witnesses, and they shall prophesy a thousand two hundred *and* threescore days, clothed in sackcloth.

4   These are the two olive trees, and the two candlesticks standing before the God of the earth.

5   And if any man will hurt them, fire proceedeth out of their mouth, and devoureth their enemies: and if any man will hurt them, he must in this manner be killed.

6   These have power to shut heaven, that it rain not in the days of their prophecy: and have power over waters to turn them to blood, and to smite the earth with all plagues, as often as they will.

7   And when they shall have finished their testimony, the beast that ascendeth out of the bottomless pit shall make war against them, and shall overcome them, and kill them.

8   And their dead bodies shall lie in the street of the great city, which spiritually is called Sodom and Egypt, where also our Lord was crucified.

9   And they of the people and kindreds and tongues and nations shall see their dead bodies three days and an half, and shall not suffer their dead bodies to be put in graves.

10   And they that dwell upon the earth shall rejoice over them, and make merry, and shall send gifts one to another; because these two prophets tormented them that dwelt on the earth.

11   And after three days and an half the Spirit of life from God entered into them, and they stood upon their feet; and great fear fell upon them which saw them.

12   And they heard a great voice from heaven saying unto them, Come up hither. And they ascended up to heaven in a cloud; and their enemies beheld them.

13   And the same hour was there a great earthquake, and the tenth part of the city fell, and in the earthquake were slain of men seven

thousand: and the remnant were affrighted, and gave glory to the God of heaven.

14 The second woe is past; and, behold, the third woe cometh quickly.

15 And the seventh angel sounded; and there were great voices in heaven, saying, The kingdoms of this world are become *the kingdoms* of our Lord, and of his Christ; and he shall reign for ever and ever.

16 And the four and twenty elders, which sat before God on their seats, fell upon their faces, and worshipped God,

17 Saying, We give thee thanks, O Lord God Almighty, which art, and wast, and art to come; because thou hast taken to thee thy great power, and hast reigned.

18 And the nations were angry, and thy wrath is come, and the time of the dead, that they should be judged, and that thou shouldest give reward unto thy servants the prophets, and to the saints, and them that fear thy name, small and great; and shouldest destroy them which destroy the earth.

19 And the temple of God was opened in heaven, and there was seen in his temple the ark of his testament: and there were lightnings, and voices, and thunderings, and an earthquake, and great hail.

Chapter 11

The Two Witnesses and Seventh Trumpet

Two Witnesses:

Here John is given a measuring rod and told to rise and measure the temple of God. Which means the temple is rebuilt at this time. This is where the man of sin, trying to be God, sits. In II Thessalonians 2:1-4 Now we beseech you, brethren, by the coming of our Lord Jesus Christ and by our gathering together unto him, That ye be not soon shaken in mind, or be troubled, neither by spirit, nor by word, nor by letter as from us, as that the day of Christ is at hand. Let no man deceive you by any means: for that day shall not come except there come a falling away first, and that man of sin be revealed, the son of perdition; Who opposeth and exalted himself above all that is called God, or that is worshipped; so that he as God sitteth in the temple of God shewing himself that he is God. Notice in verses one and two Paul is speaking about the rapture when he speaks about our gathering together unto him Jesus Christ. He is saying do not be deceived Jesus will not come until the man of sin or the Anti Christ is revealed. Also there will be a great falling away. People do not want to hear the truth. In Verse 7 Paul said that the mystery of iniquity is at work and will get worse because the thing that keeps it in check will be taken away. What keeps iniquity in check? It is the truth. Notice what is said in verse 10, because they received not the truth or a love for it to be saved God will send them a strong delusion so that they will believe a lie. Let us look at a few verses of scripture in Daniel 9:13 As it is written in the law of Moses, all this evil is come upon us: yet made we not our prayer before the Lord our God, that we might turn from our iniquities, and understand thy truth. I Thessalonians 2:13 For this cause also thank we God without ceasing, because, when ye received the word of God which ye heard of us, ye received it not as the word of men, but as it is in truth, the word of God, which effectually worketh also in you that believe. II Thessalonians 2:10-13 and with all deceivableness of unrighteousness in them that perish; because they received not the love of the truth, that they might be saved. And for this cause God shall send them strong delusion, that they should believe a lie: That they all might be damned who believed not the truth, but had pleasure in righteousness. But we are bound to give thanks always to God for you, brethren beloved of the Lord, because God hath from the beginning chosen you to salvation through sanctification of the Spirit and belief of the truth. II Timothy 4:3-4 for the time will come when they will not endure sound doctrine; but after their own lust shall they heap to themselves teachers, having itching ears; and they shall turn away their ears from the truth, and shall be turned unto fables. II Peter 2:1-2 but there were false prophets also among the people, even as there shall be false teachers among you, who privately shall bring in damnable heresies, even denying the Lord that bought them and bring upon themselves swift destruction. And many shall follow their pernicious ways; by reason of which the way of truth shall be evil spoken of. We now live in a country that was built on truth but now we hear that there is no truth. They teach evolution, a fact and Christianity as a myth. Our children are taught that there are no absolutes. Our judges do not believe in any absolutes. There is no soundness in most of their decisions. We take God out and put sin in our schools and still do not understand why good children turn bad. Jesus said I am the way, the truth and the life. So you can see truth is a person and when he is taken away sin always abounds. The Jewish people will worship in the temple and sacrifice on the altar until the temple is desecrated by the man of sin in Matthew 24:15 When ye therefore shall see the abomination of desolation, spoken of by Daniel the prophet, stand in the holy place, (whoso readeth, let him understand)

The temple court or outer court area around the temple will be given to the Gentiles as well as the holy city Jerusalem. In verse 3 we see a turn of events for the beast and those that ally with him. They are going to meet some giant opposition. God has two witnesses who will cause havoc on earth for a thousand two hundred and sixty days. These witnesses will have great power. They are called the two olive trees and also the two candlesticks or lamp stands, standing before the God of the earth. Before a thing could be considered true, there had to be at least two witnesses. Hebrews 10:28 He that despised Moses' law died without mercy under two or three witnesses. II Corinthians 13:1

this is the third time I am coming to you. In the mouth of two or three witnesses shall every word be established? They are clothed in sackcloth (garments used for mourning) but they may have put these on so that they would stand out or be different from the crowd. These are just men they can be hurt and will eventually be killed. When anyone does hurt them they are able to call fire down and devour their enemies. They are hated by the people on earth, so this is God's way of protecting them. They have a three and one half year job to do for God. This is the first half of the tribulation period because at the end of this period the beast comes from the bottomless pit with power to kill them. He then reigns for a three and one half year period himself. God has given these witnesses power that only the Old Testament prophets had. I do not believe they are Old Testament prophets. Jesus said in Matthew 11:13-14 for all the prophets and the law prophesied until John, and if ye will receive it, this is Elias, which was for to come. Matthew 17:10-13 and his disciples asked him, saying, why then say the scribes that Elias must first come? And Jesus answered and said unto them, Elias truly shall first come, and restore all things. But I say unto you, That Elias is come already, and they knew him not, but have done unto him whatsoever they listed. Likewise shall also the Son of man suffer of them. Then the disciples understood that he spake unto them of John the Baptist. They can shut Heaven or stop it from raining, power to turn water to blood and also to smite the earth with all plagues as they will. This period of time the first half of the tribulation will be war with good and evil, the saints versus the devil. God is not going to be without a witness. The saints will stand their ground but will eventually be killed with God's permission. Notice that the beast makes war with these two witnesses. I find it hard to believe that war has to be declared on just two people. These witnesses are going to be operating in Jerusalem. This is where it all takes place. Right now Jerusalem is very populated with Christians from many countries of the world. Also the Orthodox Jews will be offering sacrifices in the temple. Look what is said in Daniel 11:32-35 and such as do wickedly against the covenant shall he corrupt by flatteries: but the people that do know their God shall be strong, and do exploits. And they that understand among the people shall instruct many: yet they shall fall by the sword, and by flame, by captivity, and by spoil, many days. Now when they shall fall, they shall be holpen with a little help: but many shall cleave to them with flatteries. And some of them of understanding shall fall, to try them, and to purge, and to make them white, even to the time of the end: because it is yet for a time appointed.

Also in Daniel 7:21-22 I beheld, and the same horn made war with the saints, and prevailed against them; Until the Ancient of days came, and judgment was given to the saints of the most High; and the time came that the saints possessed the kingdom. In Revelation 13:7 and it was given unto him to make war with the saints, and to overcome them: and power was given him over all kindred and tongues, and nations. There is going to be open warfare between Heaven and hell and it is going to look like hell is going to win but in Daniel 12:7 And I heard the man clothed in linen, which was upon the waters of the river, when he held up his right hand and his left hand unto heaven, and sware by him that liveth forever that it shall be for a time, times, and an half; and when he (Anti Christ) shall have accomplished to scatter the power of the holy people, all these things shall be finished. Daniel Chapter 7 verses 26 and 27 said it best. But the judgment shall sit, and they shall take away his (Anti Christ) dominion, to consume and to destroy it unto the end. And the kingdom and dominion, and the greatness of the kingdom under the whole heaven, shall be given to the people of the saints of the most High whose kingdom is an everlasting kingdom, and all dominions shall serve and obey him. There are two witnesses on earth that bear record to God, the Church and Israel. Both are identified with the olive tree and also the candlestick. In Isaiah 43:12 I have declared; and have saved, and I have shewed, when there was no strange god among you: therefore ye are my witnesses, saith the Lord, that I am God. Also in Matthew 24:14 and this gospel of the kingdom shall be preached in the entire world for a witness unto all nations; and then shall the end come. Jews and Gentiles are both called olive trees. Romans 11 :24 for if thou wert cut out of the olive tree which is wild by nature, and wert grafted contrary to nature into a good olive tree: how much more shall these, which be the natural branches, be grafted into their own olive tree? In Chapter 11 the things that are happening are to get the attention of the Jewish people. This is primarily God's way of getting Israel's attention. There will be great distress upon that land as recorded in Daniel 12:1 And at that time shall Michael stand up, the great prince which standeth for the children of they people: and there shall be time of trouble, such as never was since there was a nation even to that same time: and at that time thy people shall be delivered, everyone that shall be found written in the book. Notice they (Jews) also have to have their name in the Book of Life. Also in Zechariah 13:8-9 And it shall come to pass, that in all the land,saith the Lord, two parts therein shall be cut off and die: but the third shall be left therein. And I will bring the third part through the fire, and will refine them as silver is refined, and will try them as gold is tried: they shall call on my name; and I will hear them: I will say, It is my people: and they shall say, The Lord is my God. This is the fire that will refine them. Most of the world is in rebellion to God. The door is closing on the Gentiles. Revelation 9:20-21 makes this quite clear. And the rest of the men which were not killed by these plagues yet repented not of the works of their hands, that they should not worship devils, and idols of gold, and silver, and brass, and stone, and of wood: which neither can see, nor hear, nor walk: Neither repented they of their murders; nor of their sorceries, nor of their fornication, nor of their thefts. We as God's people owe the Jews a great deal for getting the gospel down to us. Most of the first Jewish Christians were killed for their faith but they still remained faithful. Notice what Paul said in Romans 11:26-31 and so all Israel shall be saved: as it is written there shall come out of Zion the Deliverer, and shall turn away ungodliness from Jacob: For this is my covenant unto them, when I shall take away their sins. As concerning the gospel, they are enemies for your sakes: but as touching the election, they are beloved for the fathers' sakes. For it is written: the gifts and callings of God are without repentance. For as ye in times past have not believed God, yet have now obtained mercy through their unbelief; Even so have these also now not believed that through your mercy they also may obtain mercy. He is saying it is our responsibility as Christians to show mercy to them so they can be saved. So God is going to use us even though as a nation they do not believe Christ has come or that the church is his bride. They will come to understand by our mercy. Revelation 3:9 Behold, I will make them of the synagogue of Satan, which say they are Jews, and are not, but do lie; behold, I will make them to come and worship before thy feet, (Philadelphia church) and to know that I have loved thee.

These witnesses will be killed and their bodies will lie in the streets of Jerusalem for three and half days. The world will rejoice and make merry. Sending gifts one to another. Notice also it says the people, meaning the Jews will be in on this too. But it will be short lived for them, as we shall see. At the end of three and one half days the spirit of life from God enters into them and they stand upon their feet and great fear fell upon those that saw it. A voice from heaven tells them to come up and they ascended into heaven on a cloud.

Now the Second Woe:

In the same hour that all this is taking place Jerusalem is hit with a great earthquake. One tenth of the city falls and seven thousand people die. Now they are beginning to see that God means business. A remnant of people is scared to death and now begins to give glory to God.

One more woe to come.

When the seventh angel sounds there is a great voice in Heaven saying, all the kingdoms of the world are to become the Kingdoms of Christ and his kingdom will reign forever. This is verified by Daniel 2:44 And in the days of these kings shall the God of Heaven set up a kingdom, which shall never be destroyed: and the kingdom shall not be left to other people, but it shall break in pieces and consume all these kingdoms, and it shall stand forever. The twenty-four elders fall down on their faces and worship God because he is going to use his great power to reign over the earth. The nations do not want this. They are angry because they are losing control of things. God's wrath is soon to come. Also, time to judge the dead in order to reward them whether great or small. No one will lose his reward but those that are destroying the earth will be destroyed. The temple in Heaven is opened and the ark of his testament can be seen. In this ark are the two tables of testimony or covenant. No matter how bad things look, God will not break his covenant with Israel. The Lamb of God is going to prevail.

CHAPTER 12

AND there appeared a great wonder in heaven; a woman clothed with the sun, and the moon under her feet, and upon her head a crown of twelve stars:

2 And she being with child cried, travailing in birth, and pained to be delivered.

3 And there appeared another wonder in heaven; and behold a great red dragon, having seven heads and ten horns, and seven crowns upon his heads.

4 And his tail drew the third part of the stars of heaven, and did cast them to the earth: and the dragon stood before the woman which was ready to be delivered, for to devour her child as soon as it was born.

5 And she brought forth a man child, who was to rule all nations with a rod of iron: and her child was caught up unto God, and to his throne.

6 And the woman fled into the wilderness, where she hath a place prepared of God, that they should feed her there a thousand two hundred *and* threescore days.

7 And there was war in heaven: Michael and his angels fought against the dragon; and the dragon fought and his angels,

8 And prevailed not; neither was their place found any more in heaven.

9 And the great dragon was cast out, that old serpent, called the Devil, and Satan, which deceiveth the whole world: he was cast out into the earth, and his angels were cast out with him.

10 And I heard a loud voice saying in heaven, Now is come salvation, and strength, and the kingdom of our God, and the power of his Christ: for the accuser of our brethren is cast down, which accused them before our God day and night.

11 And they overcame him by the blood of the Lamb, and by the word of their testimony; and they loved not their lives unto the death.

12 Therefore rejoice, ye heavens, and ye that dwell in them. Woe to the inhabiters of the earth and of the sea! for the devil is come down unto you, having great wrath, because he knoweth that he hath but a short time.

13 And when the dragon saw that he was cast unto the earth, he persecuted the woman which brought forth the man *child*.

14   And to the woman were given two wings of a great eagle, that she might fly into the wilderness, into her place, where she is nourished for a time, and times, and half a time, from the face of the serpent.

15   And the serpent cast out of his mouth water as a flood after the woman, that he might cause her to be carried away of the flood.

16   And the earth helped the woman, and the earth opened her mouth, and swallowed up the flood which the dragon cast out of his mouth.

17   And the dragon was wroth with the woman, and went to make war with the remnant of her seed, which keep the commandments of God, and have the testimony of Jesus Christ.

Chapter 12

The Woman Israel

In this chapter we see a woman clothed with sun, the moon under her feet, and upon her head a crown of twelve stars. Genesis 37:9 gives us this information, and he (Joseph) dreamed yet another dream, and told it his brethren, and said, Behold, I have dreamed a dream more; and, behold, the sun and the moon and the eleven stars made obeisance to me. This is not just a woman but the nation of Israel. She is about to give birth to a man child as recorded in Isaiah 66:7 -8 Before she travailed, she brought forth; before her pain came, she was delivered of a man child. Who hath heard such a thing? Who hath seen such things? Shall the earth be made to bring forth in one day? Or shall a nation be born at once? For as soon as Zion travailed, she brought forth her children. This man child is the 144,000 who were sealed in Chapter 7. This seal is a mark for security or preservation. This 144,000 are to be preserved until they are given birth. The nation of Israel has been blinded to the gospel for 2000 years or more but now they are going to experience the new birth.

The dragon or Satan is going to try to stop this birth along with the seven nations and also the ten kingdoms he presides over. The devil has control over one third of the angels in heaven but even they will not be enough to prevent this birth. He is going to try to devour this child as soon as it is born. She brings forth a man child who will rule all nations with a rod of iron. If Satan does not stop this he will lose control over the nation. This man child will be completely undefiled with no sexual contact with women. As soon as they are born they will be taken up into heaven. There is no mention of them until Chapter 14 when they return to earth with Christ. They are the first fruits unto God and to the Lamb. There could be no rapture prior to this if they are the first fruits. The law of the first fruits was to guarantee more to come. The woman fled into the wilderness where she has a place prepared before hand for a period of a thousand two hundred sixty days. So this could not be Mary the mother of Jesus.

61

In Hosea 2:14-15 therefore, behold, I will allure her, and bring her into the wilderness, and speak comfortably unto her. And I will give her, vineyard from Thence, and the valley of Achor for a door of hope: and she shall sing there, as in the days of her youth, and as in the day when she came up out of the land of Egypt. The prophet is speaking concerning the nation of Israel. Notice verse 6 of Revelation 12.

The woman fled into the wilderness and there is war in Heaven. A phrase that does not sound true but Satan does have access to Heaven as we learn in the first chapter of Job. God is beginning to cleanse Heaven and will soon begin to cleanse the earth. There is a fight in Heaven but Michael and his angels removed the dragon and his angels to the earth where the dragon knows now that his time is short. Also he cannot accuse God's people anymore. The people on earth still overcome the devil by a good testimony and the blood of Jesus Christ, which cleanses us from all our sins. Heaven is rejoicing over the expulsion of Satan but the earth is going to feel his fury.

The Third Woe:

Notice when the devil is cast down to earth, the first thing he does is to try to destroy the woman or Israel. It is only by the divine will of God that Israel is protected. They are either flown into the place of protection, by the term two great wings, or they are moved very swiftly into this place of safety. The serpent tries to stop the woman by casting out of his mouth, waters as a flood. In scripture, water is understood to be peoples.

In Revelation 17:15 John said the waters where the great whore sits is multitudes and nations and tongues of people. Notice the earth helped the woman by opening her mouth and swallowed up the flood. Numbers 16:28-32 and Moses said, Hereby ye shall know that the Lord hath sent me to do all these works; for I have not done them of mine own mind. If these men die the common death of all men, or if they be visited after the visitation of all men: then the Lord hath not sent me. But if the Lord make a new thing, and the earth open her mouth, and swallow them up, with all that appertain unto them, and they go down quick into the pit; then ye shall understand that these men have provoked the Lord. And it came to pass, as he had made an end of speaking all these words, that the ground clave asunder that was under them; and the earth opened her mouth, and swallowed them up, and their houses, and all the men that appertained unto Korah, and all their goods. The dragon is very mad at the woman but she is under the protection of God. Now, the dragon sets his sights on the remnant of the seed of Israel, who keeps the commandments of God and also has the testimony of Jesus Christ. In Revelation 13:7-8 and it was given unto him to make war with the saints, and to overcome them: and power was given him over all kindreds, and tongues, and nations. And all that dwell upon the earth shall worship him, whose names are not written in the book of life of the Lamb slain from the foundation of the world. But in Revelation 15:2-3 And I saw as it were a sea of glass mingled with fire: and them that had gotten the victory over the beast, and over his image, and over his mark, and over the number of his name, stand on the sea of glass, having the harps of God. And they sing the song of Moses the servant of God, and the song of the Lamb, saying, Great and marvelous are thy works, Lord God Almighty; just and true are thy ways, thou King of saints. We see that the dragon's victories are short lived. This remnant keeps the commandments of God. They live by the book. They also know Jesus Christ. This remnant will endure until the rapture in Chapter 14.

CHAPTER 13

AND I stood upon the sand of the sea, and saw a beast rise up out of the sea, having seven heads and ten horns, and upon his horns ten crowns, and upon his heads the name of blasphemy.

2 And the beast which I saw was like unto a leopard, and his feet were as *the feet* of a bear, and his mouth as the mouth of a lion: and the dragon gave him his power, and his seat, and great authority.

3 And I saw one of his heads as it were wounded to death; and his deadly wound was healed: and all the world wondered after the beast.

4 And they worshipped the dragon which gave power unto the beast: and they worshipped the beast, saying, Who is like unto the beast? who is able to make war with him?

5 And there was given unto him a mouth speaking greater things and blasphemies; and power was given unto him to continue forty and two months.

6 And he opened his mouth in blasphemy against God, to blaspheme his name, and his tabernacle, and them that dwell in heaven.

7 And it was given unto him to make war with the saints, and to overcome them: and power was given him over all kindreds, and tongues, and nations.

8 And all that dwell upon the earth shall worship him, whose names are not written in the book of life of the Lamb slain from the foundation of the world.

9 If any man have an ear, let him hear.

10 He that leadeth into captivity shall go into captivity: be that killeth with the sword must be killed with the sword. Here is the patience and the faith of the saints.

11 And I beheld another beast coming up out of the earth; and he had two horns like a lamb, and he spake as a dragon.

12 And he exerciseth all the power of the first beast before him, and causeth the earth and them which dwell therein to worship the first beast, whose deadly wound was healed.

13 And he doeth great wonders, so that he maketh fire come down from heaven on the earth in the sight of men,

14 And deceiveth them that dwell on the earth by *the means of* those miracles which he had power to do in the sight of the beast; saying to

them that dwell on the earth, that they should make an image to the beast, which had the wound by a sword, and did live.

15 And he had power to give life unto the image of the beast, that the image of the beast should both speak, and cause that as many as would not worship the image of the beast should be killed.

16 And he causeth all, both small and great, rich and poor, free and bond, to receive a mark in their right hand, or in their foreheads:

17 And that no man might buy or sell, save he that had the mark, or the name of the beast, or the number of his name.

18 Here is wisdom. Let him that hath understanding count the number of the beast: for it is the number of a man; and his number *is* Six hundred threescore *and* six.

Chapter 13

The Beast from the Sea and Also out of the earth

The beast of Revelation 13:1 is the same one in Revelation 12:2-3, with the exception in Chapter 12. The crowns were on the heads of this beast. This means that the authority was given to the seven heads. Now they are on the horns. At this point in time we are entering into the last half of the tribulation period. The horns that Daniel saw on the last World Empire or Roman Empire are ten kings or kingdoms. They will rise up from the old Roman Empire with authority given to them by the other little horn that came up last and overpowered three of the original ten. Notice the description of this beast. It was like a leopard. His feet are as the feet of a bear and his mouth as the mouth of a lion. There is one thing missing, it has no head. The head has been wounded to death. This head would be the Roman Empire. The other empire was Babylon, represented by the lion. The Medo-Persian Empire represented by the bear and the Grecian Empire represented by the leopard. So from this it looks like the head of this great beast is going to be represented by the Roman Empire. The head that was wounded to death is the head of the Roman Empire. All the others are mentioned in Chapter 13:2. This one is not mentioned. When Rome came to the Zenith of its power in BC 46 until AD 180 the emperor demanded to be worshipped as god and also proclaimed themselves to be god. Not to give allegiance to them meant certain death. This is why so many Christians were killed by this government for 200 years. The Christians were so persistent in their faith even in the face of death that the empire finally succumbed to Christianity in AD 160-226. Tertullian wrote, we are of yesterday, yet we have filled your empire, your cities, your towns, your island, your tribes, your camps, castles, palaces, assemblies and senate. By the end of the imperial persecution AD 313, Christians numbered about one half the population of the

Roman Empire:

The Conversion of Constantine:

In the course of his wars with competitors, to establish himself on the throne, on the eve of the battle of Milvain Bridge, just outside Rome (October 27, A.D. 312), he saw in the sky, just above the setting sun, a vision of the Cross, and above it the words, "In This Sign Conquer." He decided to fight under the banner of Christ, and he won the battle, a turning point in the history of Christianity. Constantine granted to Christians and to all others full liberty of following that religion which each may choose. The first time this was done in history. By the persistent faith of the Christian community, this head was destroyed. It was by the word of God, which is the sword of God that this government fell. This is why the entire world wondered after the beast. It seems that he has conquered God. Now emperor worship would once again be instituted in this new world empire under the authority of the beast and the authority of the devil or Satan himself. So this part of the old Roman Empire comes alive again.

These are the nations that make up the seven head's.
Babylon is present day Iraq. Head number 1.
Medo Persia is present day Iran. Head number 2.
The Grecian Empire which was divided into four, is told in Daniel 8:21-22 and the rough goat is the king of Grecia: and the great horn that is between his eyes is the first king. Now that being broken, whereas four stood up for it, four kingdoms shall stand up out of the nation, but not in his power.

The four nations are:
1. Greece
2. Egypt
3. Turkey
4. Syria

These Nations make up six of the heads. This leaves the Roman Empire as Number 7 with its head as Italy. These seven nations will make up the seven heads of this beast that rises up in the near future.

Most of these countries are Islamic except Italy which is Roman Catholic. The dragon has given all the power to this beast and also he is worshipped along with the beast. These nations will constitute a very great army because the world can see no one that is able to defeat them. Now we see a great empire that has risen up but still no emperor. In verse 5 we see a mouth given to it. This will be the spokesman. He is the little horn of Daniel 7:21-26 I beheld and the same horn made war with the saints, and prevailed against them; until the Ancient of days came, and judgment was given to the saints of the most High; and the time came that the saints possessed the kingdom. Thus he said, the fourth beast shall be the fourth kingdom upon earth, which shall be diverse from all kingdoms, and shall devour the whole earth, and shall tread it down, and break it in pieces. And the ten horns out of this kingdom are ten kings that shall arise: and another shall rise after them; and he shall be diverse from the first, and he shall subdue three kings. And he shall speak great words against the most High, and shall wear out the saints of the most High, and think to change times and laws: and they shall be given into his hand until a time and times and the dividing of time. But the judgment shall sit, and they shall take away his dominion, to consume and to destroy it unto the end. This little horn will have the ability to unify all these nations in a one time effort to eliminate the Jew and Christian community. Notice in verse 7 it was given unto him to make war with the saints of God and also power was given him over all kindred, tongues, and nations. His power will be vast.

In verse 8 we are told that the world is in two camps: Those that worship the beast and those that have their name in the Lambs book of life. There will be no neutral ground. Notice it said all; that means everyone. If you have ears, John said you had better listen to the Word of God.

Many people will work for the beast. So if you help take people captive that opposes this system in the end you will be a captive in hell. Also if you take up arms against God's people to kill them, you will also be killed by the sword of Christ.

The first beast John saw was the world kingdom and it will be controlled by the little horn in Daniel 7:8 the beast in verse 11 is the false prophet and he exercises all the power of the first beast or he has control over the kingdom. Over this kingdom will be a delegation of great men who will operate the kingdom under the authority of the beast and the false prophet. It will have the world's best army consisting of all branches of the armed forces. The beast in verse 11 is the false prophet. He is the prime mover of the kingdom leaving the first beast free to use his army for conquering the world. He speaks like the dragon or Satan but tries to disguise himself to imitate a Lamb in order to work deception. Jesus said in Matthew 7:15 Beware of false prophets who come to you in sheep's clothing, but inwardly they are ravening wolves. This beast is a great orchestrator. He is able to put it all together but remember he is a deceiver. His great wonders are used just to deceive people who do not know the Word of God. Through his deception he is able to rally the people of earth into making an image. Notice he told them that they should make this image. So it will be a world effort creating unity among those that worship the beast.

So in effect the Roman Empire was killed by a sword, the word of God. After this image is created, the false prophet as power to give it life. This word life could mean a mind. Not necessarily to live but power to think. We already have this technology and machines that can think and also communicate. If you do not worship this image you will be killed. Remember there are just two classes of people on earth at this time. Those that worship the system and those that have their name in the Lambs Book of Life. So you can see who they are after. But they go a step farther, they are going to set up a system of identifying everyone with a mark. This mark is a badge of servitude in the Greek. So it is to identify those who serve the system. It is placed in the hand or forehead. This could also distinguish the laborers from the white collar workers. Without this identity you can neither buy or sell. The idea is to starve people out. The mark is also a series of 666's. This is the number of the beast. This is done in the wisdom of God.

CHAPTER 14

AND I looked, and, lo, a Lamb stood on the mount Sion, and with him an hundred forty and four thousand, having his Father's name written in their foreheads.

2 And I heard a voice from heaven, as the voice of many waters, and as the voice of a great thunder: and I heard the voice of harpers harping with their harps:

3 And they sung as it were a new song before the four beasts, and the elders: and no man could learn that song but the hundred *and* forty *and* four thousand, which were redeemed from the earth.

4 These are they which were not defiled with women; for they are virgins. These are they which follow the Lamb whithersoever he goeth. These were redeemed from among men, being the firstfruits unto God and to the Lamb.

5 And in their mouth was found no guile: for they are without fault before the throne of God.

6 And I saw another angel fly in the midst of heaven, having the everlasting gospel to preach unto them that dwell on the earth, and to every nation, and kindred, and tongue, and people,

7 Saying with a loud voice, Fear God, and give glory to him; for the hour of his judgment is come: and worship him that made heaven, and earth, and the sea, and the fountains of waters.

8 And there followed another angel, saying, Babylon is fallen, is fallen, that great city, because she made all nations drink of the wine of the wrath of her fornication.

9 And the third angel followed them, saying with a loud voice, If any man worship the beast and his image, and receive *his* mark in his forehead, or in his hand,

10 The same shall drink of the wine of the wrath of God, which is poured out without mixture into the cup of his indignation; and he shall be tormented with fire and brimstone in the presence of the holy angels, and in the presence of the Lamb:

11 And the smoke of their torment ascendeth up for ever and ever: and they have no rest day nor night, who worship the beast and his image, and whosoever receiveth the mark of his name.

12 Here is the patience of the saints: here *are* they that keep the commandments of God, and the faith of Jesus.

13   And I heard a voice from heaven saying unto me, Write, Blessed *are* the dead which die in the Lord from henceforth: Yea, saith the Spirit, that they may rest from their labours; and their works do follow them.

14   And I looked, and behold a white cloud, and upon the cloud *one* sat like unto the Son of man, having on his head a golden crown, and in his hand a sharp sickle.

15   And another angel came out of the temple, crying with a loud voice to him that sat on the cloud, Thrust in thy sickle, and reap: for the time is come for thee to reap; for the harvest of the earth is ripe.

16   And he that sat on the cloud thrust in his sickle on the earth; and the earth was reaped.

17   And another angel came out of the temple which is in heaven, he also having a sharp sickle.

18   And another angel came out from the altar, which had power over fire; and cried with a loud cry to him that had the sharp sickle, saying, Thrust in thy sharp sickle, and gather the clusters of the vine of the earth; for her grapes are fully ripe.

19   And the angel thrust in his sickle into the earth, and gathered the vine of the earth, and cast *it* into the great winepress of the wrath of God.

20   And the winepress was trodden without the city, and blood came out of the winepress, even unto the horse bridles, by the space of a thousand *and* six hundred furlongs.

Chapter 14

The 144,000 with Christ and the Flying Angels, Rapture and Armageddon

John said I looked and a Lamb stood on Mount Sion and with him a hundred forty four thousand with God's name written in their foreheads. In Romans 11 :26 it says, And so all Israel shall be saved: as it is written, There shall come out of Sion the Deliverer, and shall turn away ungodliness from Jacob. This great voice from heaven must have been God. But we are not told what is said. Harpers are heard harping as they sing a new song that no man could learn but the hundred forty four thousand which were redeemed from the earth. Titus 2:13-14 Looking for that blessed hope, and the glorious appearing of the great God and our Saviour Jesus Christ: Who gave himself for us that he might redeem us from all iniquity, and purify unto himself a peculiar people, zealous of good works. They are going to follow the Lamb wherever he goes. They were the first fruits unto God and the Lamb. In Romans 1 :16 Paul is saying that salvation, which is for all of God's people but in God's order is the power of God to everyone that believes, the Jew first and also the Greek or Gentile. In Proverbs 3:9 we see the law of first fruits if we want more to follow. Honor the Lord with thy substance and with the first fruits of all thine increase. Paul makes this very clear in I Corinthians 15:20-23 but now is Christ risen from the dead, and become the first fruits of them that slept. For since by man came death by man came also the resurrection of the dead. For as in Adam all die, even so in Christ shall all be made alive. But every man in his own order: Christ the first fruits; afterward they that are Christ's at his coming. This is why Christ died first and is risen to guarantee us our redemption. These groups of people are without fault before God. (Reason) as soon as they were born God takes them to Heaven. Now John sees another angel flying in the midst of Heaven having the everlasting gospel to preach to the earth, every nation, kindred and tongue and people. God is true to his word in Matthew 24:14 and this gospel of the kingdom shall be preached in all the world for a witness unto all nations; and then shall the end come. God is making sure everybody hears. This is not another gospel. This gospel is everlasting and it will never change. Galatians 1:8 but though we, or an angel from heaven, preach any other gospel unto you than that which we have preached unto you, let him be accursed. What this angel is saying in this gospel is to fear God and give glory to him and escape the judgment of hell. In verse 9-11 John is telling us that we had better not worship the beast or his system. To do so will make our fate certain in the lake of fire. There can be no repenting once we have done this. In verse 13 John hears a voice directly from Heaven saying to those that give their life they are blessed. Their labor is over and the works they have done will follow them or go with them. Jesus said in Revelation 2:26 and he that overcometh, and keepeth my works unto the end, to him will I give power over the nations. In verses 14 and 16 is the rapture of the church. We see the son of man or Jesus sitting on a white cloud having on his head a golden crown showing his authority with a sharp sickle in his hand. In Acts 1 :10-11 And while they looked steadfastly toward heaven as he went up, behold, two men stood by them in white apparel; Which also said, Ye men of Galilee, why stand ye gazing up into heaven? This same Jesus, which is taken up from you into heaven, shall so come in like manner as ye have seen him go into heaven. Jesus went up on a cloud and we see this same Jesus is coming back on a cloud. Notice that another angel came out of the temple to give the command to reap. Jesus is sitting on the cloud ready to gather his church. The angel gives him the signal because Jesus said no one knew the hour of his coming except his father who sends the angel out to tell the Lord it is time. As told in St. Mark 13:32 But of that day and that hour knoweth no man, no, not the angels which are in heaven, neither the Son, but the Father. In the parable of the wheat and tares, the wheat represents the children of God and the tares the devil. Jesus said to let both grow together-until the harvest, which is the rapture. Notice the wheat is put into the barn because in verse 15 it is said that this is the harvest. The tares are bundled to burn in Matthew 13:39-40 the enemy that sowed them is the devil; the harvest is the end of the world; and the reapers are the angels. As therefore the tares are gathered and burned in the fire; so shall it be in the end of this world. In verse 17 yet another angel comes out of the temple having a sharp sickle. But first another angel came out from the altar which had power over fire. In Revelation 6:9-11 we see the souls of them that was slain for the word of God and the testimony they held. Notice they were crying, how long Lord, Holy and true does thou not judge and avenge our blood on them that dwell on the earth. Now those souls under the altar hear the angel cry for God to begin to take vengeance on the ungodly.Notice in Revelation 13:8 it says all. That means everyone will worship the beast if their name is not written in the book of life. The winepress is the Battle of Armageddon. We see that it is Jesus who treads the Winepress alone.

CHAPTER 15

AND I saw another sign in heaven, great and marvellous, seven angels having the seven last plagues; for in them is filled up the wrath of God.

2   And I saw as it were a sea of glass mingled with fire: and them that had gotten the victory over the beast, and over his image, and over his mark, *and* over the number of his name, stand on the sea of glass, having the harps of God.

3   And they sing the song of Moses the servant of God, and the song of the Lamb, saying, Great and marvellous *are* thy works, Lord God Almighty; just and true are thy ways, thou King of saints.

4   Who shall not fear thee, O Lord, and glorify thy name? for *thou* only *art* holy: for all nations shall come and worship before thee; for thy judgments are made manifest.

5   And after that I looked, and, behold, the temple of the tabernacle of the testimony in heaven was opened:

6   And the seven angels came out of the temple, having the seven plagues, clothed in pure and white linen, and having their breasts girded with golden girdles.

7   And one of the four beasts gave unto the seven angels seven golden vials full of the wrath of God, who liveth for ever and ever.

8   And the temple was filled with smoke from the glory of God, and from his power; and no man was able to enter into the temple, till the seven plagues of the seven angels were fulfilled.

Chapter 15

Victors on the Sea of Glass, Vials for Seven Angels

John saw the seven angels having the seven last plagues and in them the Wrath of God is found. in I Thessalonians 5:9 Paul said that God hath not appointed us to wrath but to obtain salvation by our Lord Jesus Christ. So we see the church leave the wrath of God beginning. Notice John saw a sea of glass mingled with fire. In Revelation 4:6 the sea of glass is like unto crystal, very clear. This sea of glass is before the throne of God but now it has the reflection of fire in it. The word of God says that our God is a consuming fire. God is very angry with the wicked and now is ready to pour out his wrath upon them. We see those who have gotten the victory, stand on the sea of glass. They have overcome the devil by the word of their testimony and the blood of the Lamb. They loved not their lives unto death.

Now they are in Heaven while the world is suffering the wrath of God. They are singing the song of Moses and of the Lamb. The song of Moses was at the crossing of the Red Sea. In Exodus 15:1- 7 Then sang Moses and the children of Israel this song unto the Lord, and spake, saying, I will sing unto the Lord, for he hath triumphed gloriously: the horse and his rider hath he thrown into the sea. The Lord is my strength and song, and he is become my salvation: he is my God, and I will prepare him an habitation; my father's God, and I will exalt him. The Lord is a man of war: the Lord is his name. Pharaoh's chariots and his host hath he cast into the sea: his chosen captains also are drowned in the Red sea. The depths have covered them: they sank into the bottom as a stone. Thy right hand, O Lord, is become glorious in power: thy right hand, O Lord, hath dashed in pieces the enemy. And in the greatness of thine Excellency thou hast overthrown them that rose up against thee: thou sent forth thy wrath, which consumed them as stubble. Also in Revelation 5:8-10 and when he had taken the book, the four beasts and four and twenty elders fell down before the Lamb, having everyone of them harps, and golden vials full of odors which are the prayers of saints. And they sung a new song, saying, Thou art worthy to take the book, and to open the seals thereof: for thou was slain, and hast redeemed us to God by thy blood out of every kindred, and tongue and people, and nation. And hast made us unto our God kings and priests: and we shall reign on the earth. This is the song of the Lamb, one of victory and of triumph through redemption of the Lamb. After this John saw the temple open in Heaven and the seven angels came out of it with seven golden vials full of the wrath of God. The temple was filled with smoke from the glory of God and his power. Notice that no man was able to enter into the temple until the seven plagues were fulfilled; indicating that no one could make intercession to God for the earth until it was all over. No more mercy.

CHAPTER 16

AND I heard a great voice out of the temple saying to the seven angels, Go your ways, and pour out the vials of the wrath of God upon the earth.

2   And the first went, and poured out his vial upon the earth; and there fell a noisome and grievous sore upon the men which had the mark of the beast, and *upon* them which worshipped his image.

3   And the second angel poured out his vial upon the sea; and it became as the blood of a dead *man*: and every living soul died in the sea.

4   And the third angel poured out his vial upon the rivers and fountains of waters; and they became blood.

5   And I heard the angel of the waters say, Thou art righteous, O Lord, which art, and wast, and shalt be, because thou has judged thus.

6   For they have shed the blood of saints and prophets, and thou hast given them blood to drink; for they are worthy.

7   And I heard another out of the altar say, Even so, Lord God Almighty, true and righteous *are* thy judgments.

8   And the fourth angel poured out his vial upon the sun; and power was given unto him to scorch men with fire.

9   And men were scorched with great heat, and blasphemed the name of God, which hath power over these plagues: and they repented not to give him glory.

10   And the fifth angel poured out his vial upon the seat of the beast; and his kingdom was full of darkness; and they gnawed their tongues for pain,

11   And blasphemed the God of heaven because of their pains and their sores, and repented not of their deeds.

12   And the sixth angel poured out his vial upon the great river Eu-phra'tes; and the water thereof was dried up, that the way of the kings of the east might be prepared.

13   And I saw three unclean spirits like frogs *come* out of the mouth of the dragon, and out of the mouth of the beast, and out of the mouth of the false prophet.

14   For they are the spirits of devils, working miracles, *which* go forth unto the kings of the earth and of the whole world, to gather them to the battle of that great day of God Almighty.

15   Behold, I come as a thief. Blessed is he that watcheth, and keepeth his garments, lest he walk naked, and they see his shame.
16   And he gathered them together into a place called in the Hebrew tongue Ar-maged'don.
17   And the seventh angel poured out his vial into the air; and there came a great voice out of the temple of heaven, from the throne, saying, It is done.
18   And there were voices, and thunders, and lightnings; and there was a great earthquake, such as was not since men were upon the earth, so mighty an earthquake, *and* so great.
19   And the great city was divided into three parts, and the cities of the nations fell: and great Babylon came in remembrance before God, to give unto her the cup of the wine of the fierceness of his wrath.
20   And every island fled away, and the mountains were not found.
21   And there fell upon men a great hail out of heaven, *every stone* about the weight of a talent: and men blasphemed God because of the plague of the hail; for the plague thereof was exceeding great.

Chapter 16

The Wrath of God

The Vials

In verse 8 of Revelation 15 John said that no man was able to enter the temple of God until the seven vials were poured out upon the earth. So there will be no one to intercede for the people on earth. They will feel the full wrath of God. The command is given for the angels to go their way and begin to pour out their vials. The first to feel the wrath are the people with the mark of the beast and those who worship his image. They are said to have received an injurious and vicious sore. They are in very great pain. The second vial is poured out upon the sea, (it is likely to be the Mediterranean Sea) and it became congealed blood. Everything in it dies. The third vial is poured out upon the river and also the fountain or the source of the rivers. They become rivers of blood. The angel of the water congratulates God on this choice for they have shed so much blood. Notice another cries out from the altar saying, even so Lord God Almighty true and righteous are your ways. This is where the martyred saints were crying out for revenge. The fourth vial is poured out upon the sun and men are scorched with the fire. It is likely that their clothes are smoking from the great heat. They blasphemed God because they know he is responsible, but they will not repent. The fifth angel pours his vial on the seat or throne of the beast making it full of darkness. They gnawed their tongues for pain. This is from the heat of the fourth vial. The throne or tabernacle of the beast is given in Daniel 11:45 and he shall plant the tabernacles of his palace between the seas in the glorious holy mountain; yet he shall come to his end, and none shall help him. This is most likely on Mount Sinai between the Red Sea and the Mediterranean Sea. Still men can only blaspheme God because of their pains. They do not repent.

The sixth angel pours out his vial on the Euphrates River and it is dried up preparing the way for the kings of the East. Going east can take you all the way to China but it starts with Iraq, Iran, Afghanistan and Pakistan. These are Arab Nations that hate Israel. The Tigris River is just less than two hundred miles at the most from the Euphrates River, which is also a large river. John said I saw three unclean spirits like frogs come from the mouth of the dragon or Satan, the beast and the false prophet. They are the spirits of devils, which work miracles to bring the kings of all the earth with their armies to the great battle of God Almighty. A warning is given here to be ready. Jesus Will come as a thief so don't be caught naked or without the robe of righteousness. There will be no escape.

The armies of the world will gather in a place called Armageddon. Now the whole world is deceived into believing they can overthrow God. This is where Gog and all his bands come against the nation of Israel in Ezekiel in 38 and 39. Look at the two parallels of Ezekiel 38:16-23 And thou shalt come up against my people of Israel, as a cloud to cover the land; it shall be in the latter days, and I will bring thee against my land, that the heathen may know me, when I shall be sanctified in thee, O Gog, before their eyes. Thus saith the Lord God; Art thou he of whom I nave spoken in old time by my servants the prophets of Israel, which prophesied in those days many years that I would bring thee against them? And it shall come to pass at the same time when Gog shall come against the land of Israel, saith the Lord God that my fury shall come up in my face. For in my jealousy and in the fire of my wrath have I spoken, surely in that day there shall be a great shaking in the land of Israel. So that the fishes of the sea and the fowls of the heaven, and beasts of the field, and all creeping things that creep upon the earth, and all the men that are upon the face of the earth, shall shake at my presence, and the mountains shall be thrown down, and the steep places shall fall, and every wall shall fall to the ground. And I will call for a sword against him throughout all my mountains, saith the Lord God every man's sword shall be against his brother. And I will plead against him with pestilence and with blood; and I will rain upon him, and upon his bands, and upon the many people that are with him, an overflowing rain, and great hailstone, fire, and brimstone. Thus will I magnify myself, and sanctify myself; and I will be known in the eyes of many nations, and they shall know that I am the Lord. After this battle this is what God said he would do. Ezekiel 39:21-24 And I will set my glory among the heathen, and all the heathen shall see my judgment that I nave executed, and my hand that I have laid upon them. So the house of Israel shall know that I am the Lord their God from that day and forward. And the heathen shall know that the house of Israel went into captivity for their iniquity: because they trespass against me, therefore hid I my face from them, and gave them into the hand of their enemies: so fell they all by the sword. According to their uncleanness and according to their transgressions have I done unto them, and hid my face from them. We will compare them with the seventh vial. The angel poured his vial into the air and a voice from the temple said, IT IS DONE! The voices and thunder and lightening always come from the throne of God.

Revelations 16:18-20 compared to Ezekiel 39:20-23
Revelations 16:18-20

1. A great earthquake very great
2. Jerusalem was divided into three parts
3. The cities of the nations fell
4. Babylon is remembered to give her the cup of God's wrath
5. Every island fled away
6. The mountains were not found
7. Great hailstones fall from heaven

Ezekiel 38:20-23
1. A great shaking in the land of Israel
2. So great that everything is shaken
3. The mountains are thrown down
4. All steep places fall down flat
5. Every wall will fall to the ground
6. Every man's sword is against his brother
7. Pestilence and blood
8. A great rain storm
9. Great hailstones, fire and brimstone
The nation will know that God does rule.

The conclusion of Revelation 16:18-20 is given in Revelation 19:.17-21. For with the sword of his mouth he conquers all.

CHAPTER 17

AND there came one of the seven angels which had the seven vials, and talked with me, saying unto me, Come hither; I will shew unto thee the judgment of the great whore that sitteth upon many waters:

2 With whom the kings of the earth have committed fornication, and the inhabitants of the earth have been made drunk with the wine of her fornication.

3 So he carried me away in the spirit into the wilderness: and I saw a woman sit upon a scarlet coloured beast, full of names of blasphemy, having seven heads and ten horns.

4 And the woman was arrayed in purple and scarlet colour, and decked with gold and precious stones and pearls, having a golden cup in her hand full of abominations and filthiness of her fornication:

5 And upon her forehead was a name written, MYSTERY, BABYLON THE GREAT, THE MOTHER OF HARLOTS AND ABOMINATIONS OF THE EARTH.

6 And I saw the woman drunken with the blood of the saints, and with the blood of the martyrs of Jesus: and when I saw her, I wondered with great admiration.

7 And the angel said unto me, Wherefore didst thou marvel? I will tell thee the mystery of the woman, and of the beast that carrieth her, which hath the seven heads and ten horns.

8 The beast that thou sawest was, and is not; and shall ascend out of the bottomless pit, and go into perdition: and they that dwell on the earth shall wonder, whose names were not written in the book of life from the foundation of the world, when they behold the beast that was, and is not, and yet is.

9 And here is the mind which hath wisdom. The seven heads are seven mountains, on which the woman sitteth.

10 And there are seven kings: five are fallen, and one is, *and* the other is not yet come; and when he cometh, he must continue a short space.

11 And the beast that was, and is not, even he is the eighth, and is of the seven, and goeth into perdition.

12 And the ten horns which thou sawest are ten kings, which have received no kingdom as yet; but receive power as kings one hour with the beast.

13   These have one mind, and shall give their power and strength unto the beast.

14   These shall make war with the Lamb, and the Lamb shall overcome them: for he is Lord of lords, and King of kings: and they that are with him are called, and chosen, and faithful.

15   And he saith unto me, The waters which though sawest, where the whore sitteth, are peoples, and multitudes, and nations, and tongues.

16   And the ten horns which thou sawest upon the beast, these shall hate the whore, and shall make her desolate and naked, and shall eat her flesh, and burn her with fire.

17   For God hath put in their hearts to fulfil his will, and to agree, and give their kingdom unto the beast, until the words of God shall be fulfilled.

18   And the woman which thou sawest is that great city, which reigneth over the kings of the earth.

Chapter 17

The Mystery Babylon

In this chapter John is going to show the judgment of the great whore that sits upon many waters or peoples, verse 15. The kings of earth have committed fornication with her and the inhabitants of the earth have been made drunk by the wine of her fornication. The wine is the results of the actions of the kings of the earth. John said I saw a woman sitting upon the back of a scarlet colored beast full of names of blasphemy having seven heads and ten horns. When these seven heads and ten horns show up in Revelation 12-3 they were with the dragon, which is called old serpent, devil and Satan. Now they are with the beast. The devil has given the beast power over these and the woman Babylon is upon the back of the beast. The beast is using the harlot to accomplish his purpose on earth. Man is created to worship but through deception he will worship anything. The devil does not care what we worship just as long as it is not Jesus. When Jesus was being tempted by Satan. In Matthew chapter 4:8-9 the devil taketh him up into an exceeding high mountain, and sheweth him all the kingdoms of the world, and the glory of them; and saith unto him, all these things I will give thee, if thou wilt fall down and worship me, He did not accept this offer. Although Satan had the power to do it he now gives it to the Anti Christ or beast who accepts his offer, Fornication is unlawful sexual intercourse. Intercourse is a connection between persons or groups. Spiritual fornication would be unlawful spiritual intercourse or in other words the act of worshipping another god, the gods of this world. This woman is a mystery. She is called Babylon the great mother of harlots and abominations of the earth. Although from verse 18 we see that this woman is a city. New Jerusalem is also a city represented by the bride of Christ, a city that is to govern this world. Revelation 21:9-10 And there came unto me one of the seven angels which had the seven vials full of the seven last plagues, and talked with me, saying, come hither, I will show thee the bride, the Lamb's wife. And he carried me away in the spirit to a great and high mountain, and shewed me that great city, the holy Jerusalem, descending out of heaven from God. Babylon is a system of prosperity and pleasure putting man in the place of God. Defying all that oppose it; willing to kill to defend it. Built on worldly pleasure and a lust of the flesh; a government without God completely controlled by money, power, pleasure and sex with no regard of right. This woman is intoxicated with the blood of saints and the martyrs of Jesus. Meaning she gets a high from this just as people do with drugs. The angel is now going to tell John the mystery of the woman and the beast that carries her, verse 7. Notice in chapter 9:1 that a star falls from Heaven unto the earth to him is given the key to the bottomless pit. All that proceeds in this chapter come from the pit after it is opened in verse 2. Also there is an angel that rules over all of this. He is said to be a king, whose name in Hebrew is Abaddon, but in Greek it is Apollyon. Both of these names mean destroyer. Notice this angel has been locked in the bottomless pit. It is not the devil because he himself will be locked up in the pit.

Chapter 20 verse 1-2 And I saw an angel come down from heaven, having the key of the bottomless pit and a great chain in his hand. And he laid hold on the dragon, that old serpent, which is the Devil, and Satan, and bound him a thousand years. Revelation 11 :7 And when they shall have finished their testimony, the beast that ascendeth out of the bottomless pit shall make war against them, and shall overcome them, and kill them, we also see where the beast came from. In chapter 17:8 The beast that thou sawest was and is not; and shall ascend out of the bottomless pit, and go into perdition: and they that dwell on the earth shall wonder, whose names were not written in the book of life from the foundation of the world, when they behold the beast that was, and is not, and yet is. This beast could very well be one of the princes mentioned in Daniel 10:13&20 But the prince of the kingdom of Persia withstood me one and twenty days: but lo, Michael, one of the chief princes, came to help me; and I remained there with the Kings of Persia. 20 Then said he, knowest thou wherefore I come unto thee? And now will I return to fight with the prince of Persia: and when I am gone forth, lo the prince of Grecia shall come. The name Apollyon is the name in Greek of the angel in the pit of Revelation 9:11. Notice that this angel is also called a king. In Daniel 8:23, and in the latter time of their kingdom, when the transgressors are come to the full, a king of fierce countenance, and understanding dark sentences; shall stand up, this little horn is called a king also. Alexander the great moved with such great speed in conquering that his kingdom was called a leopard with four wings upon its back, Daniel 7:6. This is also the body of the kingdom that will rise up in Revelation 13:2. So this kingdom will take control over the world very fast. In Revelation 13:4 the world cries out who is able to make war with this kingdom. The great success of Alexander could be credited to the prince of Daniel 10:20. The people on earth will wonder after the beast whose names were not written in the book of life. Notice the words (were *not)* are used in this verse indicating that the book of life is closed. In Revelation 13:8 it says whose names are in the book of life, meaning the book was still open when this was written. In chapter 17:8 the only people to wonder after the beast are those who worship him. The rapture has taken place in chapter 14. In verse 9 these seven heads could mean the city of Rome which was built on seven hills. But notice in verse 1 the woman is sitting upon many waters or peoples. The seven heads could also represent the 7 kingdoms of Daniel 7, Iraq, Iran, Greece, Turkey, Syria, Egypt and Italy. These make up the seven countries also called in scripture, mountains. There are seven kings or kingdoms. Five are already fallen. One is now ruling the Roman Empire and one is to come. In Daniel 5:25-31 and this is the writing that was written, mene, mene tekel, upharsin. This is the interpretation of the thing: mene; God hath numbered thy kingdom, and finished it. Tekel; thou are weighed in the balances, and art found wanting. Peres: thy kingdom is divided, and given to the Medes and Persians. Then commanded Belshazzar and they clothed Daniel with scarlet, and put a chain of gold about his neck, and made a proclamation concerning him, that he should be the third ruler in the kingdom. In that night was Belshazzar the king of the Chaldeans slain. And Darius the Median took the kingdom, being about threescore and two years old. Daniel said that the Babylon kingdom would be divided and given to the Medes and Persians. It did not fall as such notice that Darius the Median took the kingdom. It did not fall until it became the Persian Empire. So Babylon had not really fallen. It just changed names. The five kingdoms that did fall were the Persian Empire, the Greek Empire, which was divided into (four) as told by Daniel in Chapter 8:32. So the last kingdom to come, which will rule a short time will be

Babylon. This time Babylon will be completely destroyed by the ten kings. The beast that was and is not, is the eighth, and his kingdom is made up of the seven just as they came up in one body in Revelation 13:1.

The ten horns are ten kings upon the back of the dragon. Just as the seven heads are countries and the harlot is the false religion all these are one with the dragon or Satan in his conquest for the world. These kings come from the Roman Empire since they were upon the head of the beast describing this kingdom. Right now there are more than ten with a great deal more to come next year. When the time has come, ten prevailing kings or kingdoms will appear. Because of the little horn that rises up among them and overcomes three this little horn or beast will have complete control over these ten kingdoms. Also God has put it in their hearts to destroy the city of Babylon. The Battle of Armageddon in Revelation 19:19 we see them gathered together to try and overthrow the Lord. The whore presides over a great deal of people. Just before the great battle the ten kings will destroy the whore, doing the Lord's will and leaving only the beast and his kingdom for Christ to deal with. The whore, although she compasses a large area, is also a great city; which is her headquarters. This could be Rome, since this is the head.

CHAPTER 18

AND after these things I saw another angel come down from heaven, having great power; and the earth was lightened with his glory.

2 And he cried mightily with a strong voice, saying, Babylon the great is fallen, is fallen, and is become the habitation of devils, and the hold of every foul spirit, and a cage of every unclean and hateful bird.

3 For all nations have drunk of the wine of the wrath of her fornication, and the kings of the earth have committed fornication with her, and the merchants of the earth are waxed rich through the abundance of her delicacies.

4 And I heard another voice from heaven, saying, Come out of her, my people, that ye be not partakers of her sins, and that ye receive not of her plagues.

5 For her sins have reached unto heaven, and God hath remembered her iniquities.

6 Reward her even as she rewarded you, and double unto her double according to her works: in the cup which she hath filled fill to her double.

7 How much she hath glorified herself, and lived deliciously, so much torment and sorrow give her: for she saith in her heart, I sit a queen, and am no widow, and shall see no sorrow.

8 Therefore shall her plagues come in one day, death, and mourning, and famine; and she shall be utterly burned with fire: for strong is the Lord God who judgeth her.

9 And the kings of the earth, who have committed fornication and lived deliciously with her, shall bewail her, and lament for her, when they shall see the smoke of her burning,

10 Standing afar off for the fear of her torment, saying, Alas, alas that great city Babylon, that mighty city! for in one hour is thy judgment come.

11 And the merchants of the earth shall weep and mourn over her; for no man buyeth their merchandise any more:

12 The merchandise of gold, and silver, and the precious stones, and of pearls, and fine linen, and purple, and silk, and scarlet, and all thyine wood, and all manner vessels of ivory, and all manner vessels of most precious wood, and of brass, and iron, and marble,

13   And cinnamon, and odours, and ointments, and frankincense, and wine, and oil, and fine flour, and wheat, and beasts, and sheep, and horses, and chariots, and slaves, and souls of men.

14   And the fruits that thy soul lusted after are departed from thee, and all things which were dainty and goodly are departed from thee, and thou shalt find them no more at all.

15   The merchants of these things, which were made rich by her, shall stand afar off for the fear of her torment, weeping and wailing.

16   And saying, Alas, alas, that great city, that was clothed in fine linen, and purple, and scarlet, and decked with gold, and precious stones, and pearls!

17   For in one hour so great riches is come to nought. And every shipmaster, and all the company in ships, and sailors, and as many as trade by sea, stood afar off,

18   And cried when they saw the smoke of her burning, saying, What *city* is like unto this great city!

19   And they cast dust on their heads, and cried, weeping and wailing, saying, Alas, alas, that great city, wherein were made rich all that had ships in the sea by reason of her costliness! for in one hour is she made desolate.

20   Rejoice over her, *thou* heaven, and ye holy apostles and prophets; for God hath avenged you on her.

21   And a mighty angel took up a stone like a great millstone, and cast *it* into the sea, saying, Thus with violence shall that great city Babylon be thrown down, and shall be found no more at all.

22   And the voice of harpers, and musicians, and of pipers, and trumpeters, shall be heard no more at all in thee; and no craftsman, of whatsoever craft *he be*, shall be found any more in thee; and the sound of a millstone shall be heard no more at all in thee;

23   And the light of a candle shall shine no more at all in thee; and the voice of the bridegroom and of the bride shall be heard no more at all in thee: for thy merchants were the great men of the earth; for by thy sorceries were all nations deceived.

24   And in her was found the blood of prophets, and of saints, and of all that were slain upon the earth.

Chapter 18

The Destruction of Babylon

The angels in this book vary a great deal in stature and greatness. Some are spoken as just an angel and others are spoken of in great power, some with extreme brightness and others mighty in stature. Still others are flying but all do the work of God. This angel cries mightily with a strong voice saying, Babylon the great is fallen, is fallen. This fall is given in Chapters 14, 16, 17, 18, and 19. So the fall of Babylon is very important. Her dwelling place is to become a habitation of devils and every foul spirit and a cage for every unclean and hateful bird. Notice that, (all) that means every one of the nations have been involved with her. The kings of the earth have committed fornication with her. This is not a natural act of fornication. This is a system that replaces God in this world and the kings of the nations love it. The merchants are made rich by the merchandise that flows between these nations. This is a harlot religion by the kings of earth. Nineveh was destroyed because of the multitude of the whoredoms of the well-favored harlot, the mistress of witchcraft that selleth nations through her whoredoms and families through her witchcraft. Nahum 3:4 is almost the same situation. Destruction is on the way and word is given to God's people to get out otherwise they'll be partakers of her plagues. Her sin has reached up to heaven and God has remembered her lawlessness. In Genesis 18:20-21 And the Lord said, Because the cry of Sodom and Gomorrah is great, and because their sin is very grievous; I will go down now, and see whether they have done altogether according to the cry of it, which is come unto me; and if not, I will know. Here we see the same situation. The sin of Sodom was pride, fullness of bread and abundance of idleness; neither did she help the poor or needy. This is almost the sin of our country. This woman is drunk with blood of the saints and with the martyrs of Jesus. The abominations of this woman are everywhere. An abomination is anything God hates.

Here are some things God said that were an abomination to him.
1. Graven images or idles of gods
2. To kill son's or daughters
3. Use divination or observer of times
4. Enchanters or Witches
5. Charmers to consult with familiar spirits
6. Wizard or Necromancer
7. To defraud in business in any way

Here are other scriptures you may look up. Proverbs 6:16-19, 12:22, 21:27, 28:9. According to this our entire country is an abomination to God. It may be that almost all of our great cities and those of the world could be considered Babylon cities. Look at Revelation 16:19. When the seventh seal is poured out it says that the cities of the nations fell and great Babylon also came in remembrance to give her God's wrath. This system of Babylon is in direct opposition to God and God's people. As she has done to God's people, God commanded it back to her double because she glorified herself and lived deliciously or in the lap of luxury. He turned her luxury into torment and sorrow for she is saying I am a Queen and not a widow so I shall see no sorrow. So in one day she will be judged, death, mourning, famine, and finally burnt with fire. Men want to be their own God, make their own rules, and set their own standards with total disregard to the word of God. This is why judgment is so forth coming upon this earth. The people of earth have loved this city because it was full of pleasures but now that it is being burned with fire they are lamenting, crying, and bewailing her. They do this from a safe distance for fear of her torment. The merchants do the same because of their loss of business.

Notice the categories of their merchandise.
1. Gold, silver, precious stones, diamonds, pearls, etc.
2. Fine linen, purple and scarlet
3. Ivory, thymine wood, precious wood
4. Brass, iron and marble
5. Cinnamon, odours, ointment and frankincense
6. Wine, oil, fine flour, wheat
7. Cattle, sheep

8. Horses and chariots, this is probably cars today
9. Slaves and souls of men

These are the most expensive and luxury items of the rich and famous. Now all this is gone. The merchants are weeping and wailing over this great city. John said this great city was clothed in fine linen, purple, scarlet and decked with gold, precious stones and pearls. This city has more to do with commerce and trade than anything else. In New York was the World Trade Center but now that it is gone it will be interesting to see where it will be next. This may be the reason for its fall. Remember the mark of the beast has to do with buying and selling (commerce). In one hour such great riches has come to naught. All the ships owners and the sailors that sailed them and those that do the buying and selling cried when they saw the smoke at her burning. They just can't believe that this is happening to so great a city. Completely burned up. Rejoice is the word from Heaven. God hath avenged you on her or God has done this for you. Remember her sins have reached all the way to Heaven. This great city was affecting Heaven and earth with her sins. Now Heaven is rejoicing, earth is crying. This city is being compared to a great millstone or weight upon the world. This stone is cast into the sea to signify that it is completely over for her. She will not rise again. The Lamb in Chapter 5:6 is going to conquer all of his foes. This book is about him. Every enemy will be defeated, even Satan himself in the end. Only those left standing will be the godly. What God has started in Genesis he has finished in Revelation. We are more than conquerors but only through him.

This is what is being said. Worthy is the Lamb that was slain to receive power, riches, wisdom, strength, honor, glory and blessing. If only earth had the ability to praise our Lord as they do in Heaven for all his wonderful work to the children of men. The nations were deceived by sorceries or witchcraft and deception. In her (Babylon) was found the blood of prophets and saints but also the blood of all that were slain upon the earth.

This looks like the same spirit of Babylon that Israel and all mankind was confronted with. This is recorded in Deuteronomy 13:12-16 If thou shalt hear say in one of thy cities, which the Lord thy God hath given thee to dwell there, saying, Certain men, the children of Belial, are gone out from among you, and have withdrawn the inhabitants of their city, saying, Let us go and serve other gods, which ye have not known; Then shalt thou enquire, and make search, and ask diligently and behold if it be truth, and the thing certain, that such abomination is wrought among you; Thou shalt surely smite the inhabitants of that city with the edge of the sword, destroying it utterly, and all that is therein, and the cattle thereof, with the edge of the sword. And thou shalt gather all the spoil of it into the midst of the street thereof, and shalt burn with fire the city, and all the spoil thereof every whit, for the Lord thy God: and it shall be a heap for ever; it shall not be built again. This sounds like the same situation as Babylon.

CHAPTER 19

AND after these things I heard a great voice of much people in heaven, saying, Alleluia; Salvation, and glory, and honour, and power, unto the Lord our God;

2   For true and righteous are his judgments: for he hath judged the great whore, which did corrupt the earth with her fornication, and hath avenged the blood of his servants at her hand.

3   And again they said, Alleluia. And her smoke rose up for ever and ever.

4   And the four and twenty elders and the four beasts fell down and worshipped God that sat on the throne, saying, Amen; Alleluia.

5   And a voice came out of the throne, saying, Praise our God, all ye his servants, and ye that fear him, both small and great.

6   And I heard as it were the voice of a great multitude, and as the voice of many waters, and as the voice of mighty thunderings, saying, Alleluia: for the Lord God omnipotent reigneth.

7   Let us be glad and rejoice, and give honour to him: for the marriage of the Lamb is come, and his wife hath made herself ready.

8   And to her was granted that she should be arrayed in fine linen, clean and white: for the fine linen is the righteousness of saints.

9   And he saith unto me, Write, Blessed *are* they which are called unto the marriage supper of the Lamb. And he saith unto me, These are the true sayings of God.

10   And I fell at his feet to worship him. And he said unto me, See *thou do it* not: I am thy fellowservant, and of thy brethren that have the testimony of Jesus: worship God: for the testimony of Jesus is the spirit of prophecy.

11   And I saw heaven opened, and behold a white horse; and he that sat upon his *was* called Faithful and True, and in righteousness he doth judge and make war.

12   His eyes *were* as a flame of fire, and on his head *were* many crowns; and he had a name written, that no man knew, but he himself.

13   And he *was* clothed with a vesture dipped in blood: and his name is called The Word of God.

14   And the armies *which were* in heaven followed him upon white horses, clothed in fine linen, white and clean.

15   And out of his mouth goeth a sharp sword, that with it he should smite the nations: and he shall rule them with a rod of iron: and he treadeth the winepress of the fierceness and wrath of Almighty God.

16   And he hath on his vesture and on his thigh a name written, KING OF KINGS, AND LORD OF LORDS.

17   And I saw an angel standing in the sun; and he cried with a loud voice, saying to all the fowls that fly in the midst of heaven, Come and gather yourselves together unto the supper of the great God;

18   That ye may eat the flesh of kings, and the flesh of captains, and the flesh of mighty men, and the flesh of horses, and of them that sit on them, and the flesh of all *men, both* free and bond, both small and great.

19   And I saw the beast, and the kings of the earth, and their armies, gathered together to make war against him that sat on the horse, and against his army.

20   And the beast was taken, and with him the false prophet that wrought miracles before him, with which he deceived them that had received the mark of the beast, and them that worshipped his image. These both were cast alive into a lake of fire burning with brimstone.

21   And the remnant were slain with the sword of him that sat upon the horse, which *sword* proceeded out of his mouth: and all the fowls were filled with their flesh.

Chapter 19

The Marriage Supper and Doom of Beast and False Prophet

Notice in the first verse there is a great voice of much people in Heaven giving praise, honor, glory and power to the Lord our God. He has destroyed the great whore that had corrupted the earth and again they said Alleluia. Her smoke will rise up for ever. Notice also that these are people in Heaven. Up to this point it has always been souls. Who are these people in Heaven? We will soon see. Notice that the four and twenty elders and the four beasts are still in the presence of God. They are not the saints of God. They are different. They are God's personal ministers. They have appeared all the way through the book. A command came from the throne or presence of God for all to worship God both small and great everyone. And a voice is heard like a great multitude as loud as a great waterfall or mighty thundering, saying Alleluia for the Lord God omnipotent reigneth. Notice what is said next. Let us be glad and rejoice and give honor to him (God). Notice the inset for the marriage of the lamb is come, and His (God) wife has now made herself ready. This is Israel. The lamb is getting married and God's wife Israel had made herself ready for the wedding. In Ezekiel 36:25-38 then will I sprinkle clean water upon you, and ye shall be clean: from all your filthiness, and from all your idols, will I cleanse you. A new heart also will I give you, and a new spirit will I put within you: and I will take away the stony heart out of your flesh, and I will give you a heart of flesh. And I will put my spirit within you, and cause you to walk in my statues, and ye shall keep my judgments, and do them. And ye shall dwell in the land that I gave to your fathers; and ye shall be my people, and I will be your God. I will also save you from all your uncleanness: and I will call for the corn, and will increase it, and lay no famine upon you. And I will multiply the fruit of the tree, and the increase of the field, that ye shall receive no more reproach of famine among the heathen. Then shall ye remember your own evil ways, and your doings that were not good, and shall lothe yourselves in your

98

own sight for your iniquities and for your abominations. Not for your sakes do I this, saith the Lord God, be it known, unto you: be ashamed and confounded for your own ways, O house of Israel. Thus saith the Lord God; in the day that I shall have cleanses you from all your iniquities I will also cause you to dwell in the cities and the wastes shall be builded. And the desolate land shall be tilled, whereas it lay desolate in the sight of all that passed by and they shall say, This land that was desolate is become like the garden of Eden; and the waste and desolate and ruined cities are become fenced, and are inhabited. Then the heathen that are left round about you shall know that I the Lord build the ruined places, and plant that that was desolate: I the Lord have spoken it, and I will do it. Thus saith the lord God: I will yet for this be enquired of by the house of Israel, to do it for them; I will increase them with men like a flock. As the holy flock, as the flocks of Jerusalem in her solemn feasts; so shall the waste cities be filled with flocks of men; and they shall know that I am the Lord. Here God is keeping his word to the nation of Israel to redeem them also in Isaiah 54:1-8 Sing, O barren, thou that didst not bear; break forth into singing, and cry aloud" thou that didst not travail with child; for more are the children of the desolate than the children of the married wife, saith the Lord. Enlarge the place of thy tent, and let them stretch forth the curtains of thine habitations: spare not lengthen thy cords, and strengthen thy stakes; For thou shalt break forth on the right hand and on the left; and thy seed shall inherit the Gentiles, and make the desolate cities to be inhabited. Fear not for thou shalt not be ashamed: neither be thou confounded; for thou shalt not be put to shame: for thou shalt forget the shame of thy youth, and shalt not remember the reproach of thy widowhood any more. for thy maker is thine husband: the Lord of hosts is his name; and thy Redeemer the Holy one of Israel; The God of the whole earth shall he be called. For the Lord hath called thee as a woman forsaken and grieved in spirit, and a wife of youth, when thou wast refused, saith thy God. For a small moment have I forsaken thee; but with great mercies will I gather thee. In a little wrath I hid my face from thee for a moment; but with everlasting kindness will I have mercy on thee, saith the Lord thy Redeemer. Here God is telling Israel that once again he is going not only to be their God but from this day and forward. God is saying I will be a husband to you and you will be my wife. What the nation will experience here will make her ready for the fine linen clean and white. The angel says to John write blessed are those who are called to the marriage supper of the Lamb. Now we see why in Revelation 12:14 the woman is put in a secure place for the three and one half years. Now the marriage supper of the Lamb has finally come and all the saints are In Heaven. The bride of Christ and those that are called to this is the nation of Israel. You do not send out invitations to the Bride.

She will be there so this call is to God's wife Israel. He has kept his word to rid the world of evil and Satan. He does this is in righteousness and in truth. Here he appears as John saw him in Revelation 1:14-16. He has a name that no man can know but he himself. We will never know all about God. His clothes are dripping in blood. He has already defeated his foes. Their blood is on his garments. This is already told about in Isaiah 63:1-6 who is this that cometh from Edom, with dyed garments from Bozrah? This that is glorious in his apparel, traveling in the greatness of his strength? I that speak in righteousness, mighty to save. Wherefore art thou red in thine apparel, and thy garments like him that treadeth in the winefat? I have trodden the winepress alone; and of the people there was none with me: for I will tread them in mine anger, and trample them in my fury; and their blood shall be sprinkled upon my garments, and I will stain all my raiment. For the day of vengeance is in mine heart, and the year of my redeemed is come. And I looked, and there was none to help; and I wondered that there was none to uphold; therefore mine own arm brought salvation unto me; and my fury it upheld me. And I will tread down the people in mine anger, and make them drunk in rny fury, and I will bring down their strength to the earth. Out of his mouth goes a sharp sword. This is the word of God. The nations will be ruled by God's word and they will be conquered by the word. In fact it was written before the world began. From here and forward He will be KING OF KINGS and LORD of LORDS. The first time Jesus came back it was *on* a white cloud to gather the saints. Here he is coming back on a white horse. He's the one the Anti Christ tries to imitate in chapter 6:1. This is the true Christ. He is faithful and true and he only makes war in righteousness. His eyes were as a flame of fire. He is not going to let anyone escape his judgment. An angel standing In the sun cries out to the whole world for the vultures and fowls to get ready to eat because most of the world is about to be slain. Notice in verse 19, all the world and its powers can do is just to assemble itself for the battle and there is none, The beast and false prophets are taken and put directly into the lake of fire, which is the second death. Notice the beast and false prophets are taken and put directly into the lake of fire and brimstone and when the devil is also cast in one thousand years later, they are still there. In Hebrews 9:27 And, as it is appointed unto men once to die, but after this the judgment. And also in II Peter 2:9 The Lord knoweth how to deliver the godly out of temptations, and to reserve the unjust unto the day of judgment to be punished. From this we see that all men will be judged before being punished but these two were put directly into the lake of fire. So were they merely men? The remnant were slain with the sword of Jesus and they were given to the fowls. This explains what happens here very well. In Ezekiel 39:17-22 And, thou son of man, thus saith the Lord God; Speak unto every feathered fowl and to every beast of the field, assemble yourselves, and come; gather yourselves on every side to my sacrifice that I do sacrifice for you, even a great sacrifice upon the mountains of Israel, that ye may eat flesh, and drink blood. Ye shall eat the flesh of the mighty and drink the blood of the princes of the earth, of rams, of lambs, and of goats, of bullocks, all of them fatlings of Bashan. And ye shall eat fat till ye be full, and drink blood till ye be drunken, of my sacrifice which I have sacrificed for you. Thus ye shall be filled at my table with horses and chariots, with mighty men, and with all men of war, saith the Lord God. And I will set my glory among the heathen, and all the heathen shall see my judgment that I have executed, and my hand that I have laid upon them. So the house of Israel shall know that I am the Lord their God from that day and forward. From this we can see that Israel will once again be exalted to her place of supremacy. The ungodly will be dirt under her feet and from this day and forward Israel will reign as the greatest nation on earth.

CHAPTER 20

AND I saw an angel come down from heaven, having the key of the bottomless pit and a great chain in his hand.

2   And he laid hold on the dragon, that old serpent, which is the Devil, and Satan, and bound him a thousand years,

3   And cast him into the bottomless pit, and shut him up, and set a seal upon him, that he should deceive the nations no more, till the thousand years should be fulfilled: and after that he must be loosed a little season.

4   And I saw thrones, and they sat upon them, and judgment was given unto them: and I *saw* the souls of them that were beheaded for the witness of Jesus, and for the word of God, and which had not worshipped the beast, neither his image, neither had received *his* mark upon their foreheads, or in their hands; and they lived and reigned with Christ a thousand years.

5   But the rest of the dead lived not again unto the thousand years were finished. This *is* the first resurrection.

6   Blessed and holy *is* he that hath part in the first resurrection: on such the second death hath no power, but they shall be priests of God and of Christ, and shall reign with him a thousand years.

7   And when the thousand years are expired, Satan shall be loosed out of his prison,

8   And shall go out to deceive the nations which are in the four quarters of the earth, Gog and Ma'gog, to gather them together to battle: the number of whom *is* as the sand of the sea.

9   And they went up on the breadth of the earth, and compassed the camp of the saints about, and the beloved city: and fire came down from God out of heaven, and devoured them.

10   And the devil that deceived them was cast into the lake of fire and brimstone, where the beast and the false prophet *are*, and shall be tormented day and night for ever and ever.

11   And I saw a great white throne, and him that sat on it, from whose face the earth and the heaven fled away; and there was found no place for them.

12   And I saw the dead, small and great, stand before God; and the books were opened: and another book was opened, which is *the book* of life: and the dead were judged out of those things which were written in the books, according to their works.

13   And the sea gave up the dead which were in it; and death and hell delivered up the dead which were in them: and they were judged every man according to their works.

14   And death and hell were cast into the lake of fire. This is the second death.

15   And whosoever was not found written in the book of life was cast into the lake of fire.

Chapter 20

Binding of Satan, First and Second Resurrection, Judgment

We do not read any where in the book after Chapter 9 that the door to the pit is shut. But another angel has the key and also the chain to bind Satan for a thousand years. There is no mistaking who this is. He is called old serpent, dragon, devil and Satan. In verse 4, we see thrones and people sitting upon them. These are the disciples in Matthew 19:27-28 Then answered Peter and said unto him, Behold, we have forsaken all, and followed thee; what shall we have therefore? And Jesus said unto them, Verily I say unto you, That ye which have followed me in the regeneration when the Son of man shall sit in the throne of his glory, ye also shall sit upon twelve thrones, judging the twelve tribes of Israel. Notice another group of people here. They are called souls of men that were beheaded for the witness of Jesus and for the word of God and which had not worshipped the beast or his image neither had received his mark upon their foreheads or in their hand. Notice that all these people were not killed but all had overcome. Listen to what Jesus said in Revelation 3:20-22 Behold, I stand at the door and knock: if any man hears my voice, and opens the door, I will come in to him, and will sup with him, and he with me. To him that overcometh will I grant to sit with me in my throne, even as I also overcame, and am set down with my Father in his throne, He that hath an ear, let him hear what the Spirit saith unto the churches. These are the people of the last church of the seven. (Laodicean).The word lived here means to be made alive again. These are people that will be in the Millennium. Verse 5 said the rest of the dead would not be made alive again until the thousand years are expired. These cannot be the wicked dead because they will never live again. Romans 6:23 For the wages of sin is death; but the gift of God is eternal life through Jesus Christ our lord. This is true again in John 11:25-26 Jesus said unto her, I am the resurrection, and the life: he that believeth in me, though he were dead, yet shall he live; And whosoever liveth and believeth in me shall never die.

Believest thou this? Lets put it another way. In John 3:36 He that believeth on the Son hath everlasting life: and he that believeth not the Son shall not see life; but the wrath of God abideth on him. John makes this very plain that the wicked dead will never live. This is the First Resurrection. John said that the second death had no power over them. They are alive for evermore and will be priests of God. The job of a priest is to take the thing of God and show it to men. There will not be another resurrection for a thousand years. The curse will be lifted. Men will live to be very old. Jesus will rule from Jerusalem. This will be the Capitol of the world. This reign will be a rod of iron. Revelation 2;26-27 And he that overcometh; and keepeth my works unto the end, to him will I give power over the nations. And he shall rule them with a rod of iron; as the vessels of a potter shall they be broken to shivers; even as I received of my Father. We see that the church and the 144,000 will participate. Revelation 12:5 and she brought forth a man child, who was to rule all nations with a rod of iron: and her child was caught up unto God, and to his throne. All that is not in the first resurrection will be raised at the second one of Revelation verse 12. After this period of time Satan will be freed and will immediately go out to again deceive the world. The number is as the sands of the seashore. This is why the world, was ruled by a rod of iron. Satan was bound but the heart of man is still corrupt. It was just as after the flood the wicked were killed off but it only took a few years until man began to rebel against God (The Tower of Babel). Almost all the world with the devil himself goes to overthrow the city of God, (Jerusalem) but they are all consumed by fire.

The devil is again apprehended but this time he is put into the lake of fire. Notice the beast and false prophet are still there. They are not burned up. Now, a great white throne, it is judgment time. The earth and the Heavens fled away from him that sat on the throne. All creation is suspended in space ready for judgment. Notice the question was asked in Revelation 6:17 it asks who will be able to stand? There are two groups of people to be judged here, those in verse 12 and those in verse 13.

This is the last day; the Day of Judgment. After this, time will be no more. We will go into eternity with a new Heaven and a new earth.

To see who will stand in this judgment look at Psalms 1:4-5 the ungodly are not so: but are like the chaff which the wind driveth away. Therefore the ungodly shall not stand in the judgment, nor sinners in the congregation of the righteous. The first things we see at the first judgment are the dead standing before God. The books (plural) were opened which will be deeds of the saints and the other the book of life. Here is where we see just how good our works were. I Corinthians 3:12-15 Now if any man build upon this foundation gold, silver, precious stones, wood, hay, stubble; Every man's work shall be made manifest: for the day shall declare it, because it shall be revealed by fire; and the fire shall try every man's work of what sort it is. If any man's work abides which he hath built thereupon, he shall receive a reward. If any man's work shall be burned, he shall suffer loss; but he himself shall be saved; yet so as by fire. This day will be ruined for many. Their works did not stand the test; though they are saved. For others it will be a day for crowns. I said that this is the last day judgment. Notice what Jesus said in John Chapter 6:39, 40, 44 and 54. And this is the Father's will which hath sent me, that of all which he hath given me I should lose nothing, but should raise it up again at the last day. And this is the will of him that sent me, that everyone which seeth the Son, and believeth on him may have everlasting life: and I will raise him up at the last day. No man can come to *me,* except the Father which hath sent me draw him and I will raise him up at the last day. Whoso eateth my flesh, and drinketh my blood, hath eternal life; and I will raise him up at the last day. This word (last) in the Hebrew means the final, in place or time, the very end. In John 12:48 Jesus said he that rejecteth me, and receiveth not my words, hath one that judgeth him; the word that I have spoken, the same shall judge him in the last day. So these are the righteous dead. In the second resurrection in verse 13 the sea gives up its dead. This is not the sea of water. When people are buried at sea or lost at sea, the sea does not keep them. They go either to be with the Lord or to Hell. This *is* why so many people after death are cremated and their ashes thrown into the ocean. They think God cannot find them. This is the sea of lost humanity. At the end of the thousand years all others are in hell and will be delivered up to stand trial; notice there are no books. They have no good works nor are their names in the Book of Life. Yet they will be judged by their works on earth in respect to knowledge of

God's word and evil deeds performed. In Luke 12:47-48 and that servant, which knew his Lord's will and prepared not himself neither did according to his will shall be beaten with many stripes. But he that knew not and did commit things worthy of stripes shall be beaten with few stripes. For unto whomsoever much is given, of him shall be much required; and to whom men have committed much, of him they will ask the more. We see how this will work. Death, the last enemy to be conquered is finally put into the lake of Fire. Also hell now becomes the Lake of Fire, the final end. If your name is not In the Book of Life then into the Lake of Fire you go. This judgment is mentioned in John 12:48-as told in the above paragraph.

CHAPTER 21

AND I saw a new heaven and a new earth: for the first heaven and the first earth were passed away; and there was no more sea.

2   And I John saw the holy city, new Jerusalem, coming down from God out of heaven, prepared as a bride adorned for her husband.

3   And I heard a great voice out of heaven saying, Behold, the tabernacle of God *is* with men, and he will dwell with them, and they shall be his people, and God himself shall be with them, *and be* their God.

4   And God shall wipe away all tears from their eyes; and there shall be no more death, neither sorrow, nor crying, neither shall there be any more pain: for the former things are passed away.

5   And he that sat upon the throne said, Behold, I make all things new. And he said unto me, Write: for these words are true and faithful.

6   And he said unto me, It is done. I am Alpha and Omega, the beginning and the end. I will give unto him that is athirst of the fountain of the water of life freely.

7   He that overcometh shall inherit all things; and I will be his God, and he shall be my son.

8   But the fearful, and unbelieving, and the abominable, and murderers, and whoremongers, and sorcerers, and idolaters, and all liars, shall have their part in the lake which burneth with fire and brimstone: which is the second death.

9   And there came unto me one of the seven angels which had the seven vials full of the seven last plagues, and talked with me, saying, Come hither, I will shew thee the bride, the Lamb's wife.

10   And he carried me away in the spirit to a great and high mountain, and shewed me that great city, the holy Jerusalem, descending out of heaven from God,

11   Having the glory of God: and her light *was* like unto a stone most precious, even like a jasper stone, clear as crystal;

12   And had a wall great and high, *and* had twelve gates, and at the gates twelve angels, and names written thereon, which are *the names* of the twelve tribes of the children of Israel:

13   On the east three gates; on the north three gates; on the south three gates; and on the west three gates.

14   And the wall of the city had twelve foundations, and in them the names of the twelve apostles of the Lamb.

15   And he that talked with me had a golden reed to measure the city, and the gates thereof, and the wall thereof.

16   And the city lieth four-square, and the length is as large as the breadth: and he measured the city with the reed, twelve thousand furlongs. The length and the breadth and the height of it are equal.

17   And he measured the wall thereof, an hundred *and* forty *and* four cubits, *according to* the measure of a man, that is, of the angel.

18   And the building of the wall of it was *of* jasper: and the city *was* pure gold, like unto clear glass.

19   And the foundations of the wall of the city *were* garnished with all manner of precious stones. The first foundation was jasper; the second, sapphire; the third, a chalcedony; the fourth, an emerald;

20   The fifth, sardonyx; the sixth, sardius; the seventh, chrysolyte; the eighth, beryl; the ninth, a topaz; the tenth, a chrysoprasus; the eleventh, a jacinth; the twelfth, an amethyst.

21   And the twelve gates *were* twelve pearls; every several gate was of one pearl: and the street of the city *was* pure gold, as it were transparent glass.

22   And I saw no temple therein: for the Lord God Almighty and the Lamb are the temple of it.

23   And the city had no need of the sun, neither of the moon, to shine in it: for the glory of God did lighten it: and the Lamb *is* the light thereof.

24   And the nations of them which are saved shall walk in the light of it: and the kings of the earth do bring their glory and honour into it.

25   And the gates of it shall not be shut at all by day: for there shall be no night there.

26   And they shall bring glory and honour of the nations into it.

27   And there shall in no wise enter into it any thing that defileth, neither *whatsoever* worketh abomination, or *maketh* a lie: but they which are written in the Lamb's book of life.

Chapter 21

The New Heaven and New Jerusalem

In this Chapter eternity begins. The last day has ended. As Jesus said in John 12:48 the days of judgment is over. In verse 11 John said I saw the Heaven and earth go away and there was found no place for them. So it looks like the wicked dead will forever be on the old earth to drift around in eternity. No place was found for them. In Isaiah 65:17-25 for, behold, I create new heavens and a new earth: and the former shall not be remembered, nor come into mind, But be ye glad and rejoice for ever in that which I create: for, behold, I create Jerusalem a rejoicing, and her people a joy. And I will rejoice in Jerusalem, and joy in my people: and the voice of weeping shall be no more heard in her, nor the voice of crying. There shall be not more thence an infant of days, nor an old man that hath not filled his days: for the child shall die an hundred years old; but the sinner being an hundred years old shall be accursed. And they shall build houses, and inhabit them; and they shall plant vineyards, and eat the fruit of them. They shall not build, and another inhabit; they shall not plant, and another eat: for as the days of a tree are the days of my people, and mine elect shall long enjoy the work of their hands. They shall not labour in vain, nor bring forth for trouble; for they are the seed of the blessed of the Lord, and their offspring with them. And it shall come to pass, that before they call, I will answer; and while they are yet speaking, I will hear. The wolf and the lamb shall feed together, and the lion shall eat straw like the bullock: and dust shall be the serpent's meat. They shall not hurt nor destroy in all my holy mountain, saith the Lord. From this it looks like God will push a reset button on our minds and the old life will never be remembered again. Heaven could not be the place of splendor if we could remember the fate of our unsaved loved ones. Here we see a new Heaven and a new earth. Again he said the first heaven and the first earth were passed away. Also now there is no more sea. This is probably the Mediterranean Sea. The New Jerusalem will be almost 1500 hundred miles in four directions. This is to make room for it. John said I saw the holy city, New Jerusalem coming down from God out of Heaven prepared.

Jesus said I go to prepare you a place. So the Lord kept His promise. This city is like a bride. Another voice cries out, behold the tabernacle of God with men and he (God) will dwell with them and they shall be his people; Notice it says God himself. The God no one could look upon or even approach unto, now is in the middle of his people. All the things that have brought tears to our eyes will be gone along with every pain. In fact, all things will be made new. This is a faithful saying. The Alpha and Omega, the first and last will give everyone who is thirsty water from the fountain of life. Remember what Jesus said to each of the seven churches about, he that overcometh. Well, they that did will become God's sons. We will see now what a small price we paid for such a great blessing. Those that did not overcome will now be overcome with fire and brimstone, which is the second death. Most people never thought that it would come to this. The world really ended and people were judged for their sins and sent into eternal punishment. We hear it all the time. God would never do this to people he created. Well they have done it to themselves the way that they live. Fearful, unbelieving, abominable, murders, whoremongers, sorcerers, idolaters and last of all everyone who was a liar have sealed their fate. One of the seven angels says to John, come here I will show you the bride, the Lamb's wife, having the glory of God and her light was like a stone most precious, even a jasper stone, clear as crystal. In Heaven there will be no gray areas. Everything will be perfectly clear.

This city had a great high wall with twelve gates and an angel at every gate. Every gate was named after the twelve tribes of Israel. There were three gates on every side and the wall had twelve foundations and in every foundation the name of one of the apostles of Jesus. Notice the way into this city was by going through a gate and each gate represented one of the twelve tribes. These sons of Jacob were born about 1700 years before Christ. They also remain today. Their nation has suffered more than any. Some suffered from their own sins but also so much from a world that hated them. Remember what Jesus said, salvation is of the Jews. In my lifetime millions have been killed just because of that name. So we owe the Jews for our entrance into the city. Look at what is supporting the city. The foundations are represented by the twelve apostles. But remember they were the

111

foundations of the early church. Most were martyred for their faith in God. This nation gave us Jesus and He gave the world the church. He said I will build my church. We as Gentiles came along after everything was in place. In fact, Jesus said I have prepared a great supper and everything is ready, just come!

I guess that is why there are not any names like Baptist, Methodist, Church of God, Assembly of God or any other Gentile name. We owe so much to this nation. We should thank God for them. This city is 1500 miles wide, the length is the same and so is the height. The wall sitting on the foundations is jasper. So you could see right through the wall, it will be clear as crystal. Also the street was pure gold like clear glass. The glory of God will reflect through this city so that His light will be everywhere. Each foundation is a precious stone. The first jasper then sapphire, a chalcedony, emerald, sardonyx, sardius, chrysolyte, beryl, topaz, chrysoprasus, jacinth and amethyst. And the twelve gates were twelve pearls; every several gate was of one pearl: and the street of the city was pure gold. There will be no need for a Temple. It is just a place to worship God from a distance. Here God will be in our midst and will be the object of our worship directly.

There will be no need for the sun or moon. The glory of God will shine in this city brighter than the sun. The nation of them that are saved will have access to this city. Also the kings will bring their glory and honor into it. This also is told in Zechariah 2:10 sing and rejoice, O daughter of Zion: for, lo, I come, and I will dwell in the midst of thee, saith the Lord. Night will pass away in this city and the gates will always be open. All the glory and honor of all the nations will be an offering to God. There will be one eternal day without one sorrow. What a day this will be just to be forever in the presence of God and the Lamb. There will be nothing to defile this city in any way. And all that enter will be by written invitation only. Get your name in this book. Have your sins washed away by the blood of Christ.

CHAPTER 22

AND he shewed me a pure river of water of life, clear as crystal, proceeding out of the throne of God and of the Lamb.

2   In the midst of the street of it, and on either side of the river, *was there* the tree of life, which bare twelve *manner of* fruits, *and* yielded her fruit every month: and the leaves of the tree *were* for the healing of the nations.

3   And there shall be no more curse: but the throne of God and of the Lamb shall be in it; and his servants shall serve him:

4   And they shall see his face; and his name *shall be* in their foreheads.

5   And there shall be no night there; and they need no candle, neither light of the sun; for the Lord God giveth them light: and they shall reign for ever and ever.

6   And he said unto me, These sayings *are* faithful and true: and the Lord God of the holy prophets sent his angel to shew unto his servants the things which must shortly be done.

7   Behold, I come quickly: blessed *is* he that keepeth the sayings of the prophecy of this book.

8   And I John saw these things, and heard *them*. And when I had heard and seen, I fell down to worship before the feet of the angel which shewed me these things.

9   Then saith he unto me, See *thou do it* not: for I am thy fellowservant, and of thy brethren the prophets, and of them which keep the sayings of this book: worship God.

10   And he saith unto me, Seal not the sayings of the prophecy of this book: for the time is at hand.

11   He that is unjust, let him be unjust still: and he which is filthy, let him be filthy still: and he that is righteous, let him be righteous still: and he that is holy, let him be holy still.

12   And, behold, I come quickly; and my reward *is* with me, to give every man according as his work shall be.

13   I am Alpha and Omega, the beginning and the end, the first and the last.

14   Blessed *are* they that do his commandments, that they may have right to the tree of life, and may enter in through the gates into the city.

15 For without *are* dogs, and sorcerers, and whoremongers, and murderers, and idolaters, and whosoever loveth and maketh a lie.

16 I Jesus have sent mine angel to testify unto you these things in the churches. I am the root and the offspring of David, *and* the bright and morning star.

17 And the Spirit and the bride say, Come. And let him that heareth say, Come. And let him that is athirst come. And whosoever will, let him take the water of life freely.

18 For I testify unto every man that heareth the words of the prophecy of this book, If any man shall add unto these things, God shall add unto him the plagues that are written in this book:

19 And if any man shall take away from the words of the book of this prophecy, God shall take away his part out of the book of life, and out of the holy city, and *from* the things which are written in this book.

20 He which testifieth these things saith, Surely I come quickly. Amen. Even so, come, Lord Jesus.

21 The grace of our Lord Jesus Christ *be* with you all. Amen.

Chapter 22

Conclusion and Final Prayer

John said I saw a pure river of water of life clear as crystal coming out of the throne of God and the Lamb. This is a great river. In the midst of it is a street of pure gold. This street is in the middle of the river with a row of trees in the middle of the street that give life. Also on both sides of the river is a row of trees of life. These trees bear twelve manners of fruits and yield fruit every month. The leaves of the trees are for the healing of the nations. The curse on mankind started by eating fruit from the wrong tree. We will never be tempted again. God has a cure for all the nations, the leaves of these trees. Man was cursed in the garden and here the curse is lifted. God himself will be in our midst and now we will serve him forevermore. John keeps telling us about the light of the city and how we will reign forever. It seems almost too good to be true. But He said these sayings are faithful and true because God had shown it to him by His angels. Before you know it or even before you are ready these things will happen. Time is very short and the end is very near. Listen to the last message. Behold I come quickly. Blessed are those who are ready. John said I wanted to worship the angel that showed me these things but he said do it not. Worship God. This book is not to be sealed up for the time is at hand. If you are unjust by the time all this has happened you will always be an unjust person. If you are filthy then you will forever be filthy: But on the other hand if you are righteous, praise God you will always be righteous. The same goes if you are holy.

Listen to this warning: behold I come quickly and my reward is with me to give every man according as his work shall be. When Jesus comes for his people if you are righteous you will be rewarded for your righteousness. If you are ungodly then you will be cast into the lake of fire. Don't think you can get ready after Jesus comes back because there will be no one left behind who could ever make themselves ready. In St. Matthew 25 remember the five foolish virgins who came afterwards saying Lord, Lord open to us. But He answered and said, verily I say unto you, I know you not. Watch therefore, for ye know neither the day nor the hour wherein the Son of man cometh. Again Jesus said I am Alpha and Omega, the beginning and the end. If you don't deal with Jesus at first; then you will have to deal with him in the last. There are many blessings in this book. If you keep His commandments you will have a right to the tree of life by going through the gates of this city. Those that are locked outside are dogs, sorcerers, whoremongers, murderers, idolaters and everyone who is involved with lying.

Jesus said I have sent mine angel to testify unto you these things in the church. Jesus was saying that the church needs to know these things. If the church is not going to be involved with these things, then why tell them so? Here is another invitation the spirit and the bride says come. If you hear this, you need to come. If you are thirsty you need to come. And anyone that comes can get a drink of water of life. There is a warning to all that read anything into this book or that leaves anything out. If you add to God's word then God will add to you the plagues of this book. If you take away from God's word then He will take your name out of the Book of Life. Jesus is saying surely I come quickly.

Amen.

Even So Come Lord Jesus!

May God be gracious to you, Amen.

Remember Romans 8:35-39 Who shall separate us from the love of Christ? Shall tribulation, or distress, or persecution, or famine, or nakedness, or peril, or sword? As it is written, for thy sake we are killed all the day long; we are accounted as sheep for the slaughter. Nay, in all these things we are more than conquerors through him that loved us. For I am persuaded that neither death nor life nor angels, nor principalities, nor powers, nor things present, nor things to come. Nor height, nor depth, nor any other creature, shall be able to separate us from the love of God which is in Christ Jesus our Lord. Amen!

Some Concluding Remarks #1

In the book of Revelation we are told that a great kingdom is coming and will rule all the earth through a person called the beast or Anti Christ. Here is what is said in Revelation 13:7 And it was given unto him to make war with the saints and to overcome them. And power was given him over all kindred, all tongues and all nations. This also means our country, the USA. Although we are the most powerful nation now, forces are very much at work to cause us to fall. And WE WILL FALL! The Bible tells us that the last seven years before the Millennium, world power will be shifted to the European nations of the old Roman Empire. Daniel 11:36 And the king shall do according to his will; and he shall exalt himself, and magnify himself above every god, and shall speak marvelous things against the God of gods, and shall prosper till the indignation be accomplished: for that that is determined shall be done. There will be no one to stop him until Christ comes back. We hear people talk about the events after the rapture as though we will have plenty of time to get ready. No where in the scriptures can this be found. The Bible always stresses the fact that today is the day of salvation. When the door on the Ark was shut no one else got on board. When Lot went out of Sodom, no one else was saved. When the five foolish virgins came back after the door was shut they could not get back in. The devil would like nothing better than to have you think this. People even think that if you give your life, then you will be saved. This is not true; even though a lot of people will give their life. The only thing that can save you is the blood of Christ. Our own blood has no power to save. The church is not Israel. The church is made up of Jews that have accepted Christ. But Israel as a nation will rise to her full potential as the world power when the church is with the Lord. Israel will be a nation on earth forever. Ezekiel 34:11-16, and 23-31 For thus saith the Lord God; Behold, I, even I, will both search my sheep, and seek them out. As a shepherd seeketh out his flock in the day that he is among his sheep that are scattered; so will I seek out my sheep, and will deliver them out of all places where they have been scattered in the cloudy and dark day. And I will bring them out from the people, and gather them from the countries, and will bring them to their own land, and feed them upon the mountains of Israel by the rivers, and in all the inhabited places of the country. I will feed them in a good pasture, and upon the high mountains of Israel shall their fold be: there shall they lie in a good fold and in a fat pasture shall they feed upon the mountains of Israel. I will feed my flock, and I will cause them to lie down, saith the Lord God. I will seek that which was lost, and bring again that which was driven away, and will bind up that which was broken, and will strengthen that which was sick; but I will destroy the fat and the strong; I will feed them with judgment. And I will set up one shepherd over them, and he shall feed them, even my servant David; he shall feed them, and he shall be their shepherd. And I the Lord will be their God, and my servant David a prince among them; I the Lord have spoken it. And I will make with them a covenant of peace, and will cause the evil beasts to cease out of the land: and they shall dwell safely in the wilderness, and sleep in the woods. And will make them and the places round about my hill a blessing; and I will cause the shower to come down in his season; there shall be showers of blessing. And the tree of the field shall yield her fruit, and the earth shall yield her increase, and they shall be safe in their land and shall know that I am the Lord, when I have broken the bands of their yoke, and delivered them out of the hand of those that served themselves of them. And they shall no more be a prey to the heathen, neither shall the beast of the land devour them; but they shall dwell safely, and none shall make them afraid. And I will raise up for them a plant of renown, and they shall be no more consumed with hunger in the land, neither bear the shame of the heathen anymore. Thus shall they know that I the Lord their God am with them, and that they even the house of Israel, are my people, saith the Lord God. And ye my flock, the flock of my pasture, are men, and I am your God, saith the Lord God.

Concluding Remark #2

If you cannot believe the Bible, then God has given to the world the Nation of Israel as a testimony to what He is doing. Israel is a type of time clock to let the world know where we are in relationship to the end of this age. World War II was used by God to call attention to the Jewish nation for the purpose of re-gathering them back into their land. The Jews were a nation without a home or a country. The great persecution and slaughter of the Jews by Hitler created world sympathy for them. In 1948 they were given back a portion of their own country. This has never been done before, a people brought back home after 2000 years. For over fifty years the Jews have been coming home to Israel, but in the last few years places could not be found for them fast enough to settle in. This is spoken of in Deuteronomy 30:3-5 That then the Lord thy God will turn thy captivity, and have compassion upon thee, and will return and gather thee from all the nations, whither the Lord thy God hath scattered thee. If any of thine be driven out unto the outmost parts of heaven, from thence will the Lord thy God gather thee, and from thence will he fetch thee: And the Lord thy God will bring thee into the land which thy fathers possessed, and thou shalt possess it; and he will do thee good, and multiply thee above thy fathers.

Concluding Remark #3

II Thessalonians 1:1-8 Here Paul is saying that Jesus is going to come back and we will be gathered to him (the Rapture.) He also said not to be troubled in spirit or by some word. Neither by a letter as though it was from him, that the day of Christ was at hand or the Rapture was at hand. He said not to be deceived by no means about this. He said that day would not come until there was a great falling away first and the man of sin be revealed (the son of perdition.) Also this man cannot come until the falling away and people no longer want to hear the truth. This is where we are at today in this country. So in effect what Paul is saying is that at the Rapture will not come until this man comes on the scene.

Concluding Remark #4

This was told fifteen hundred years before Christ and about 2500 years from today. Jerusalem is now the controversy of the world and will grow even more intense. This also is told in Zechariah 12:1-3 The burden of the word of the Lord for Israel, saith the Lord, which stretcheth forth the heavens, and layeth the foundation of the earth, and formeth the spirit of man within him. Behold, I will make Jerusalem a cup of trembling unto all the people round about, when they shall be in the siege both against Judah and against Jerusalem.

And in that day will I make Jerusalem a burdensome stone for all people: all that burden themselves with it shalt be cut in pieces, though all the people of the earth be gathered together against it. This was told about five hundred years before Christ.

Concluding Remark #5

In I Thessalonians 4:-13.::18 in verses 13 and 14 Paul is saying those that sleep or died believing in Christ would come back with God. These are the saints that have died up to the beginning of the seven years tribulation. From verse 15 to verse 18 he is talking about those that are killed or come through the first three and one half years.

Notice what Paul said about these. The Lord himself would descend from Heaven and the dead in Christ would rise first. Then those that are alive and remain would be those that lived until the rapture. Then he said the living and the dead would meet him in the air and they would forever be with the Lord. The saints in verse 14 will remain with God in Heaven for 1000 years. The rest would be with Jesus for the 1000 years or the Millennial Reign in Jerusalem.

About the Author

He was saved in the Church of God in 1965. He worked with the Army Chaplain while on duty in Italy even before his salvation. He was a member of the Church of God until about 1990 where he took many courses that were equivalent to college credits. He has taught the Bible for almost forty years. Since 1990 he has taught an adult Bible class in Claypool Hill, Virginia.

For the past twenty years he has studied the book of Revelation, taking many notes. He also listened to Bible tapes on Revelations as he worked in his shop everyday. He has also read many books on Revelations.

Printed in the United States
22270LVS00001B/337-414

9 781418 400583